Praise for Tom Dickerson's
Priceless Gifts for All Seasons

"Tom will have you chuckling, nodding your head in knowing agreement, or even reaching for the Kleenex to dab away some tears." Lisa Lohman

"I want you to know, I really loved this. It was inspiring and uplifting." Jerri Garcia, author

"Those were a lot of stories and I enjoyed them." Laura Lewis, author

"A broad assortment of adults, children and family create encounters that will bring a smile of gratitude to the readers face." Shirley Fessel, author

PRICELESS GIFTS
FOR ALL SEASONS

TOM DICKERSON

Dedication

Priceless Gifts for All Seasons is dedicated to God and all the others mentioned in each story.

I also want to give a special thanks to all the writers critique groups in Kansas City and my writing coach and editor, RJ Thesman. Together, we write words to touch the souls of humanity.

Table of Contents

PRICELESS GIFTS
GIFTS
FOR ALL SEASONS

CHAPTER ONE

SUMMER

When Small Becomes Big

I was conquering my gambling problem and now engaged to be married. Then it happened.

Despite the highest evaluation I ever had, my employer of eighteen years in Overland Park, Kansas, let me go.

I was fifty-one and could not find related work in the Kansas City area. I applied for a job as a claims manager at John Morrell. We relocated to Sioux City, Iowa. We knew no one — no support system. A casino was a neighbor north along the Missouri River. What could I do to keep me away from temptation?

I asked myself, what brings me joy? Hearing my children say three words, "Do it again."

The words always involved something good. Laughter or smiles were often involved for both them and me followed by a sense of contentment.

This was what I needed to do. Get involved with a child.

I became a mentor for Kimanni Thompson through the Big Brother Big Sister program with a goal to spend an hour a week with him. A small use of my time to divert attention away from the casino. Maybe I could also help Kimanni stay out of trouble.

Throughout our visits, I soon realized Kimanni enjoyed his time spent with me. The feeling was mutual. I stayed away from the casino. More importantly, I learned the joy of service.

The best way to forget the past is to serve in the present.

My belief in the Big Brother Big Sister program was now so strong I encouraged others to join.

They were having a fundraiser at a Pizza Ranch in Sergeant Bluff, Iowa. *What a great way to support them and who does not like pizza?*

A worker approached me. "We're the primary sponsor this year for United Way. I need someone to say a few words at our event. Would you be willing to help?"

"What should I talk about?"

"Explain about a time you spent together with your Little Brother and how being a Big Brother has affected you."

I was terrified at the thought of speaking in front of such a large audience.

Years earlier, my supervisor recruited me to speak about United Way in front of our small claims department. My boss thought it could help my career development. Feeling helpless, I prayed, and God gave me words to say. The speech went well, and we set a record pledge drive.

Now at another place in time with a different commitment and a different heart, I wanted to speak despite my fears. The audience needed to feel the experience of being a Big Brother. My faith in God turned to prayer asking for His words to flow through me. He led me to speak about true fishing episodes involving Kimanni and other children. The words were well-accepted.

After the speech, I drove Kimanni back to school. I felt larger than the Missouri River to my west and as high as the sunlit sky above. It was as if I had discovered my purpose in life — to touch the souls of humanity.

On behalf of Big Brothers Big Sister, I spoke on two separate occasions in later years. In 2013, the Iowa Mentoring Partnership and the Iowa Commission on Volunteer Services awarded me The Excellence in Mentoring Award. The award is the most prestigious honor a mentor can receive. Karen, and Kimanni accompanied me to the award presentation at the state capital in Des Moines, Iowa. Congratulatory letters were received from House Representative Steve King and Governor Terry Branstad. Photos and a decorative glass award were presented at the State Capital, Rotunda Hall with photos to memorialize the celebration.

Today when I look back, I realize how small acts of kindness can reap big rewards. The curio cabinet in our living room holds the recognition plaque as it is among my most prized possessions.

A Lesson Through Fishing

Is it possible to catch fish without reeling them in?

Two adults fished. Each had the opportunity to maximize their catch by utilizing the following:

One box of worms shared by the two.

Five rods and reels divided between the anglers.

Three children, ages five, ten and eleven.

The first angler boasted about being a great fisherman and chose one of the five rods and reels. It was her rod and reel. New line, new reel, new rod — a real beauty. She decided to fish alone.

The second angler decided to let the three children fish. He took the four remaining rods and gave each child their own rod. He kept the remaining rod as a backup in the event of equipment failure. He baited the hooks, removed the fish, cast an occasional line for the five-year-old, and gave out wise advice.

The first angler immediately caught a couple of blue gills. She cast again and her hook set into the log near shore. As she yanked the rod to get her hook free, her string became a tangled mess. She quit fishing, content with her catch of two fish.

The second teams ten-year-old was smiling ear to ear catching another bass. He called her the Great Bass Fisherman. The eleven-year-old took a liking to large bluegill, catching the most fish. The five-year-old caught the first crappie. They filled the stringer to over-flow, letting the rest go. The wise old angler never reeled a fish in, yet he had a harvest beyond expectation.

The five-year-old went home and told his mom about the fishing trip. The following Thursday we had dinner with his mother and heard about the great trip. To this day, the three children remember the trip, and all asked to go again.

We have a choice. Will we be stingy with resources, short on time and selfish with talent?

Will we be generous with our resources, time, and talent?

This trip only took an hour.

The rods were Grandpa's who died, and the worms cost a couple of dollars.

My talent was fishing, although it was ten years since I had last fished.

Fears of failure about relating to children made no difference.

We are all part of a great family with diverse talents. If each of us gives like the wise angler, just think how much our world is blessed.

Children are waiting for a mentor. So, take a kid fishing. Teach a child how to fish. You both will find joy in a wonderful harvest.

Tippy Got it Right

After a stressful day at work, the Tahoe was a sultry ninety when I started for home. Kimanni caught me at the side door just off the deck and swimming pool.

"Can we go swim before dinner? I want to go fishing. Can we go?"

I gave that slow compromising response, "We`ll see."

We`ll see? I`ll decide. Can I keep up with this kid?

"Slow down." Kimanni ate the Jambalaya as if it were five minutes to sunset.

"Once you finish, we`ll go fishing."

The longer we wait, the cooler it will get. The humidity will be terrible by the pond.

We started for the pond. I glanced down the gravel road and saw cattle. *The rancher must have some damaged fence.* I stopped to call the property owner. She called the renter to take care of the cows. The momentary delay was not going to stop us.

The clear water brought solitude and slowed the pace for the first time that day. Then the phone rang. It was my wife, Karen.

"You`ve got to come home. The cows are drinking the chlorinated pool water. I think there might be a bull. Could they die from the water?"

Does she think I`m a herdsman, a rancher, a farmer? What can I do?

"Honey, it`s okay. I called Gail. She called the rancher. Everything will be okay. Just stay in the house."

A blue gill larger than my hand greeted the first cast. Then an eighteen-inch bass met the net at the shoreline. My watery bliss ended with a full stringer.

The journey across the pasture took us back home to fillet our fish just before nightfall. Our border collie, Tippy, wanted to have her fish and eat it, too. She was quick to respond to my command, "Kennel." It represented sixteen years of security for her, so why not go?

I was new at filleting fish, so with the time approaching ten I showered and rushed to sleep.

Morning arrived with breakfast ready. "I love biscuits and gravy. Where`s Tippy?"

"I don`t know, haven`t seen her."

"Oh no! I left her in the kennel." Forgetfulness got the best of me.

My personal comfort consumed me. I left her without food, water and without a chance to relieve herself. As I opened the door to the kennel there was no barking, no biting, and no running away from me. Forgiveness was the price of my forgetfulness.

I left for work with Tippy at the heels of my wife. Her tail wagged side to side as if sweeping away last night . She seemed content, living out her life silently, lovingly, faithfully, consistently giving us protection, loyal beyond expectations.

Can a dog be a gift from God to show us how to accept and live with one another?

Dilemmas of a Two-Year Old

After our daughter had given Owen his bath for the night, I found my way to the front porch to sit quietly before day met nightfall.

Our two-year-old grandson, now mastering the art of opening doors, decided to come out and see me. As I rocked contentedly, he joined me at another rocker. But his rocking pushed the limits.

He jumped up and down and bounced to his heart's delight. Maybe it was his version of a thrill ride. I watched as Momma joined us and said, "Owen, be careful."

Soon he found his way along the front steps, picking a yellow tulip from the flowerbed.

Momma scolded him. "Owen, you don't pick flowers from Grandpa's flower garden. Tell him you're sorry."

"Sorry, Grandpa."

"Sorry for what? Tell Grandpa you're sorry for picking the flower. Tell him you will not do it again."

It must be difficult for a two-year-old. Many a youngster picks a dandelion and Mom immediately gives a hug, kiss, or words of gratitude. Now Owen is scolded for his loving act.

The front yard soon exploded with the winged fireworks of lightning bugs. Owen was on the chase in his bare feet. So much for the bath. He waved his hands frantically as if he were on a clap-and-destroy mission.

Soon Momma captured a few lightning bugs of her own, Owen looked heavenward as the lights of the night took flight. On another day, they would find their home in a mason jar.

The evening got the best of me. After all, it is a parent's job to scold and a grandparent's job to love and hold. I held Owen's hands and slowly closed them. We set our friend free to entertain us again.

Momma gave the command, "Owen, it's time for bed."

To which I said, "Owen, I love you."

"I love you too, Grandpa."

This old man turned young again and silently gave thanks.

God, thank you for moms, toddlers, warm summer nights and bugs that light up our lives on front porches across this great land. Amen.

Dad

Dad, thank you for your example of hard work — something I inherited from you. I remember the sacrifice of time you made for us by working a second job so you could provide for life's needs while never going into debt.

Those long hours later helped me with promotions and better salary adjustments, even put me into a management position. You taught me that doing your best is a road to success.

Thank you for opportunity. You provided a financially stable home where a boy could grow to play the sports of the day. Later you provided educational opportunities, contributing to four college educations. Your men all have well-paying careers.

I remember encouraging words of hope through times of failure. You gave me optimism. After I struck out or missed a field goal, you always encouraged me.

You often boasted about the successes, the victories, of better days to come. Your words meant the world to me. Now I share words of encouragement with others, the same as you did for me.

Dad, thank you for your example of honesty, reliability, and the boldness to stand for what you believed in. Taking a stand sometimes led to confrontation, but more importantly, it led to respect. You were a man of integrity.

I am so thankful for your marriage. You and Mom lived the biblical principal, "Love binds us together in perfect harmony."

It was you, Mom, and God. Even above faith and hope is love. Both of you always loved me.

After I wrote this essay, I shared it with my wife. I started to say, "I would give anything to have just one day…." Then I became tongue-tied, the rest of my sentence trapped in emotion.

I walked to my office and whispered, "Dad I miss you." Tears flowed.

Later, I composed myself and finished the sentence. "Wouldn`t you give anything just to have one more day together with your mom and dad?"

A beauty is in God`s design, as two together are better than one. With their love, my parents became one. With their four sons — eventually the six of us and God, became a magnificent seven.

The Father`s Moment

In 2011, I found myself angry with God. I questioned his impact in my life and specifically my impact on others.

Did I have any impact on the child I mentored? If I wasn`t affecting his life, how many other lives could I influence before I died? God did not seem very alive in me.

I shared my frustration with a small Bible study group. They tried to encourage me.

"You can`t look at it that way. You`re planting seeds. Your words make a difference."

I had my doubts.

I recalled a Bible verse that indicated I should listen to wise counsel. So, I prayed for an opportunity to make a difference in someone`s life.

Father God forgive me for any wrong I`ve committed against you or others. Please provide me an opportunity to minister to someone. Amen.

The next Sunday a guest in our home wanted to go to church with Karen, Kimanni and me. We decided to let her borrow one of our cars so she could leave at her convenience. This left an empty seat in our car.

Two bridges span the Missouri River. Kimanni suggested we take the bridge farthest to the south. Construction was taking place on the bridge, but not on Sundays.

As we neared our turn, we crossed paths with a young man on the side of the road. He was a Native American with tattered blue jeans and a white t-shirt. He looked to be around twenty years old.

"Do you want a ride?" Karen asked. "Can we help get you to where you're going?" He accepted my wife's invitation.

I asked, "What's your name? Where you going?"

Chalman answered, "Can you take me to the bridge?"

I nodded. "I need to drop my wife off at church. She sings in the choir. They practice an hour before church. I can take you after dropping her off. It's not out of the way."

It was Father's Day so I offered, "I guess you're going to see your dad."

"No."

"Where's he live?"

"Michigan," he answered in disgust. "I haven't talked to him in years."

My conversation seemed to cause him pain. My heart ached for Chalman as if I had removed a scab before healing. I wished I could make it up to him.

I dropped Karen at the front door of the church.

"Would you like to go to breakfast with us? I always take Kimanni for the big "B" which stands for breakfast."

"I don't know."

"Have you eaten?"

"No."

"We all have to eat. It'll be our treat."

"Okay."

We put in our order at the Hy-Vee counter. Bacon sizzled on the grill. The aroma's smell made my mouth salivate. We sat at an isolated table where we could talk.

"Where you from?"

"Michigan, Las Vegas, Winnebago. I live with my mom on the reservation at Winnebago. I'm the first in my family to complete high school. I did it for mom, dad, and everyone I`m related to. I enrolled in college. I was supposed to start a job today. No one appreciates what I`ve done. I do everything at home, the cooking, the cleaning, and the laundry. Others do nothing. I had an argument with Mom and slammed the door. The glass shattered. I left and now I'm here. I prayed something good would happen to me today."

Then he said something that caught me off guard.

"It's finally good to see a Christian act like a Christian. I prayed I would see God today and now I have."

Before my biscuits and gravy arrived. I prayed.

"Father, I don`t know much about this man or his circumstances. It sounds to me like he's a good man. With this problem going on between Chalman and his dad, I pray you will make it right. I also pray that things might go better between Chalman and his mom. Father, if it can`t be, I still thank you that you are my father and Chalman's father and that you love both of us. I pray he knows you love him and that your will for his life might be fulfilled. He`s special. You knit him in his mother's womb. Your word says he`s made in your image, precious, honored and loved. Thank you for him. Amen."

Tears began to flow from Chalman`s eyes as if some burden had been lifted. We finished with small talk.

I invited Chalman to Sunday School. He accepted our offer to attend the class Karen and I taught. He chose a different seat for the sermon. After church, he visited with a member or two. We caught up with him and left for the bridge.

"Do you have money you could lend me?"

"No, but if you`re hungry we'll buy you something at McDonalds. We can go in or get carry out, whichever you like." The McDonalds was a block away from the bridge.

"I`ll get it to go."

We drove through and left him near the bridge.

"I`m gonna' give you my phone number. If you ever need help, call me."

The next Tuesday the phone rang.

"Hey, It`s Chalman. I just want to thank you. You saved my life."

"I don`t know what you`re talking about. I was just doing what any Christian would do."

"No, you don`t understand. I was going to the bridge to jump. You saved my life. I`ve got a new place to stay and I`m enrolled in school."

Tears rolled down my face.

A chill came over my body, but I composed myself.

"That`s great. I wish you well. Call if we can ever help."

I thought about Chalman most every day and often wondered what became of him. Then I heard a wonderful ending to the story. One of my church friends told me Chalman accepted Christ on Sunday, Father`s Day.

Generation Gap

It was a short time and a great time. Anyone watching realized there was no generation gap between a Grandfather and his grandchild.

In the summer of 2009 Karen's cousin Jeanene visited us with her mother Joyce and husband Terry, daughter Andrea and three-year-old son Caleb. Twelve-year-old Kimanni was with us. This was a weekend to forget about the trappings of work and burdens of a single mother. It was a time to relax in the dell for Caleb's first fishing trip at our neighbor's five-acre pond.

That night we lit a crackling fire with marshmallows and s'mores. Stories of present and past took center stage in the cool night.

"Every time we fish at Gail's pond, we catch blue gill larger than your hand and sometimes bass beyond fifteen inches in length. We also run out of worms. I pray for a successful and fun fishing trip. God has not let me down. I think it's divine intervention."

Terry turned his head slightly and gave a snide smile, his way of kindly saying, *I want to believe you but I'm not sure I do.*

"I'll call the owner of the pond after church tomorrow and see if we can fish again."

I slept well, waking early Sunday morning to cook and cook some more: biscuits and gravy, eggs fried and scrambled, toast, sausage, tea, coffee, and juice.

"Caleb, do you know what this is?"

My mouth dropped in astonishment at his answer. "Smorgas-bord."

We left for church. The message was short but profound. Don`t get your religion from others when you can get the message firsthand from the Bible.

We ate leftovers and headed for the pond. Kimanni led Caleb. They walked hand in hand, swinging their arms, like Andy Griffith relived.

Kimanni said, "Follow me, I'll show you a fishing trip of a life-time."

I was proud of him for leading and of Caleb for following and trusting his friend.

Upon arrival, Grandpa Terry took over. He baited the hook and cast the line between the algae and shore. A blue gill larger than his hand devoured the worm. A bass struck the next cast before the worm could reach the bottom.

Grandpa`s hands assisted Caleb as he caught a green monster. A bit of algae encased the largemouth bass and made it nearly impos-sible to get the fish to shore. The tape registered eighteen inches, a definite keeper, but it was catch and release today. The third cast was another blue gill larger than the first one.

Before the fourth, Caleb resisted, "Grandpa, can we go now?"

What was he thinking?

We took plenty of pictures and video to memorialize his first fish-ing trip.

We left to enjoy the balance of the day at the pool and sat at the table watching the children swim. Terry said, "I wasn`t sure whether to believe you or not when you told me how good the fishing was."

"Sometimes you have to experience it before you believe it."

At the campfire that next year, looking at Caleb and then the rest of us, Terry chimed in. "Do you remember when I showed you how to catch The Green Monster?"

I looked at Terry with a puzzled grin and answered for Caleb. "What Green Monster?"

Caleb and the rest of us laughed. We all remembered.

Good "F`s"

Is there such a thing as a good "F"?

She came with low expectations and left with a story to tell. Nicole was the youngest of my friend Mic`s three daughters. Cute, petite, and not afraid to speak her mind.

I asked, "Do you think we`ll catch fish today?"

Her lips tightened. She squinted and said, "I never catch anything."

How sad! Just wait and see what happens.

The night gave condensation to the morning. The girls' cowboy boots kept them dry in the seventy-degree day. We saw large blue gill as we approached the five-acre pond.

"Can you hand me the worms? "I baited the hook and threw a cast out for the young lady who now had a bit of confidence.

I handed her the rod.

"Notice how the line isn't straight. If the line begins to straighten, pull the rod up in a jerking motion, but not so hard to pull the worm from the mouth of the fish."

The line straightened. The jerk came. "I`ve got him. I`ve got a fish." The reeling came easy. Her exuberance continued. She jumped up and down with excitement, "Daddy, Daddy, I caught a fish."

Her father Mic chimed in, "Now hold on. Just hold on a minute. I want to get your picture."

As the worms began running low, the two older girls held their own. At one point, they all had a fish at the same time. Mic rushed back and forth to take photos and capture memories. Life was more about them than him.

The successful fishing trip was almost over as I baited the last hook. I noticed a large bass come to the surface, the largest of the day. "Here, take the rod." The last chapter of the fishing trip was Mic`s.

Before his crowd of four, he cast within inches in front of the largemouth. The fight was on. Strangely, the large fish offered little resistance as Mic reeled it near shore. Then, to everyone`s surprise, a fish popped out of the mouth of the bass.

"I caught the blue gill. Can you believe that? The bass had the blue gill but was never hooked. That`s why I reeled him in so fast."

The largemouth swam away to be caught another day.

We met the wives on the deck. "Mommy, Mommy, I caught twenty fish."

There was no official count.

I thought about her first remark, about never catching anything. In the past, she had experienced failure fishing and "F`s" that led to frustration.

Perhaps she could now focus on victories and the areas of life that bring joy: a firm foundation in God, family, and friends. A joyous smile in the fellowship of sharing her fishing trip over food cooked on a grill at the home of a new friend.

How might life change without the "F's"? If she had caught her fish alone, who would have shared in her joy? What if there was no family? What if there were no friends? What if there was no God in her life and no fun fellowship? What if there was no faith in her future?

These were the good "F's" of the day which brought joy and contentment. My day was filled to overflowing with the joy of serving friends.

Later, my wife asked, "What`d you think of our day?"

"You know, I`m tired, a good tired. I had great clean fun with great people fishing at a great pond God and my neighbor let me have for a morning. We caught a lot of fish. The fellowship and food were excellent. We should do it again. It was fabulous."

An Unusual Picture Day

My ordinary day for this seven-year-old was soon to change. It was the summer of 1962.

I arose as usual with one exception. I wore a crisply ironed white shirt. Picture day at school came once a year. It was supposed to be a wonderful day.

The morning started in a usual fashion with my stay-at-home mom calling, "It`s time for breakfast." I didn`t need coaxing as I could smell the savory maple syrup. I puckered my lips and raised my tongue to assure I tasted every sweet drop.

Before I left, my mother said, "Keep that shirt clean. Don`t get it dirty. I love you." As if I needed a reminder. This was my second go-around at picture day.

It was warm enough not to seek shelter in the bus stop shed near the creek. Before the bus came, the vine overhanging the creek called for me to have some fun. The narrow brown vine seemed strong enough to hold my fifty-seven-pound frame. I gave it a yank downward to assure its strength.

Off I went, soaring six feet over the creek when I heard a snap. Suddenly I was no longer airborne. I landed in the muddy water below, the shirt now a wet brown.

I was hurt. Not a physical hurt, but mental anguish as fear set in. Now what would I do? I had only one white shirt. I did the only thing my guilty seven-year-old brain could think of. I hid in the woods to avoid what was to come.

My mom and dad had this agreement regarding punishment. Mom would catch us doing something wrong and she would tell us, "Your father will deal with this when he gets home."

My father was not a flexible man. More than once, he said, "Your mother would never lie."

This meant there would be no discussing the situation. I would get a spanking.

He was a tough man with a swift firm hand, the heavyweight champion on his naval ship. He put the fear of God into me. I had felt those strong repeated stinging blows from his belt. The offenses would never be repeated for the terrifying thoughts of another spanking.

I trembled in fear, wondering how the punishment might be magnified this time to fit the crime of ruining picture day.

Time seemed to stand still in the forest. No answers. Hope was gone. What should I do? I had to face the truth.

Returning to Mom with tears, I said, "I`m sorry. I didn`t mean it."

There was something different this time as she started laughing. Laughing! This was not a laughing matter.

"Dad`s gonna' spank me."

"It`s okay. I love you. He doesn`t need to know." She gave me a security hug. At age seven, I had just discovered my lifelong best friend.

Later as an adult, I told the story to my six-year-old grandson.

He told me, "Grandpa, don't be scared. Jesus loves you, even when you`re muddy."

Three Mentor's Night

We all want the opportunity to go somewhere special. For the poor, that opportunity may never come. Poor children may never experience the joy of watching a professional baseball game.

How can we help them experience what we often take for granted?

I took Kimanni, my Little Brother from the Big Brother Big Sister program to his first semi-professional baseball game with the Sioux City Explorers. As I approached his house, Kimanni waited in the front yard.

As we entered the baseball park, we slowed to a sudden pause. Kimanni stared at the souvenir stand. I could sense his awe. Was it the excitement of never seeing such a tempting display or was it the belief Tom would not buy anything? Perhaps it was both.

I had a better seventh inning plan.

We walked the short climb of steps to see the field and stands. Across the third base side was a couple from our church with two girls, not their own. It made me happy to know they took the time to invest in a couple of lives on a cool Friday night.

Soon the game was on with the frivolity of small-town semi-professional baseball. It was t-shirt night. Throughout the game, vendors came by to throw a t-shirt to the most enthusiastic fan. None found their way to Kimanni, though his exuberance was obvious. Between innings, he caught a Twin Bing, a local candy tossed by one of those same vendors.

After the seventh inning, he asked to go to the grassy area behind the first base bleachers to chase down a foul ball.

A short time later, he ran up the bleacher steps. "I did it. I got the ball. Did you see it? Did you see me run down the ball and beat those other kids to it?"

I gave Kimanni a high five and said, "Great job."

During the late innings, I struck up a conversation with the tattooed man behind me. He shared his adolescent trouble, his adult trouble, his drug trouble, his prison time. He was 31, now with a steady job, now trying to become a good dad. His three sons and their two cousins were with him. He told me about prison and about missing his children. Sadly, all were on a Big Brother waiting list.

He talked about life no longer being about him. He gave up friends, his criminal past, his drinking. Now he was a good model for his children and their cousins.

The children obviously loved and respected him . He asked me twice about my name. I took the entrance ticket and scribbled my number. "In case you ever want to talk."

I handed my leftover kettle corn to them.

The father responded, "You can eat it now. Tell the man thank you."

"Thank you, thank you, thank you, thank you, thank you."

As we left, I said, "You kids be good. You`ve got a great dad. Obey him and your mother."

For one night, the couple from church, the prisoner set free, and I united to give the best gift the night could offer, our time and love with children.

The Explorers lost. The kids had fun. The three of us won.

The Man with Duct Tape Shoes

Can you judge a man by his shoes?

On my way home from Council Bluffs, Iowa, I picked up a hitch-hiker. The heat pushed a humid hundred degrees.

"I`m Tom. What's your name?"

"Sam."

"Where you going?"

"I need to get to Montana before getting back to my home in Ventura, California. Are you a Christian?"

"Yes.", I turned down the volume on the Christian radio station.

"I knew it. On this trip, I spent a night with a Christian biker gang that let me do some drumming for them. It was cool. A priest drove 70 miles out of his way to get me to a better highway to help me save time."

How could I help him?

Sam came with a backpack and a cane.

"You can use the cane for defense."

What kind of trouble had he seen?

He finished the sentence. "But I`ve never had to use it."

Sam and I had our differences. I have short parted hair and the portly stomach one gets from working twelve-hour days, sometimes eating on the road with no physical exercise.

He was a tall chiseled man that came from walking all day. Sam had a wide bright white smile with perfect teeth. His long blond hair flowed past his beard and ended in natural curls that bounced off his shoulders. He looked like the stereotypical Jesus or a hippy.

Rugby and surfing the oceans were his sports while I was a football kicker and could barely swim. Sam appeared to be in his mid-twenties while I was sixty.

My living was handling insurance claims with my company car while using my computer and phone. Sam had no phone or computer. He was presently unemployed. In his last job, he worked for his single father who owned a tree-cutting business.

"We just had a fierce storm split a tree," I said. "The large limbs might fall on the Morton Building that protects our cars. My neighbor, Doug, can fix anything, but we decided we need an expert for this one."

The thought of Sam helping me with the tree did cross my mind, although no further discussions took place while in the car.

The day was nearing an end with two hours of daylight left. After calling my wife Karen, we decided to offer Sam a night's stay, perhaps a shower, and some food before tomorrow's continued journey. He was appreciative, accepting my offer of free lodging.

We arrived at our country home. Although I had not suggested it Sam asked about the tree. I had not asked him to do this. In less than a minute, he checked out the chain saw. "It needs a spark plug."

This kid knows what he's doing.

"We can get it down by hand," he said, referring to my dull rusty handsaws. In the heat, I was not enthusiastic, but Sam insisted.

I walked to the side of the Morton building to get a ladder. When I returned, Sam was no longer grounded. He was up the tree like a squirrel after hickory nuts.

My role was that of gopher for saws and ropes. Sam tied off limbs and sawed away portions at a time. Large limbs were lowered slowly by the ropes with no damages sustained to the building.

I looked upward for the next limb and noticed Sam's duct-taped shoes, the original a mundane gray and the second layer a brighter purple. Was Sam poor, frugal, or both?

As the final limb came down I didn't care. But I did not forget and wondered about those shoes.

Karen joined us near the pool. We shared sweet Iowa deer jerky and summer sausage to satisfy the evening's taste buds.

Karen's sense of nurturing kicked in and Sam was led to call his mother, to tell her he was safe. Sam's mom asked to talk to Karen to confirm that everything was fine. In one phone call, we gained another friend.

Sam referred to us as angels.

I quickly replied, "Are you sure you're not the angel? You gave your time and talent without asking for anything."

I wanted to give Sam a pair of my best shoes, but they did not fit. The next day we repaid a bit by breakfast out and new shoes. Sam wanted to pay half. I refused his kind offer. We sent him off with new shoes, some jerky and summer sausage for the trip ahead.

He left with the bed sheets in place, leaving our home and property better than when he had arrived.

As we sent Sam to his next destination, he said, "We gotta' get our hugs. A tear slowly fell down my face.

Was it a tear of thanksgiving or loss that I might never see him again?

"Keep doing what you're doing," Sam said.

Tongue-tied with emotion, I wanted to repeat those words to him. But the words never came.

The Strange Cats Perfect Weekend

Our friend Sam has called Karen and me "Strange Cats." He thinks we are different.

I don't mind being called a strange cat, but I prefer Tom or Christian.

Many people complain that Christians talk a big game but their actions don't line up with their beliefs. A friend of ours named Matt says Karen and I are different. Kimanni has also made the same statement.

It always makes me sad that others who attend churches give us a bad name. Are the people they refer to really Christians? Are we Christians strange cats? What is a strange cat?

One-night Sam's mom called. He wanted to come see us. He hitchhiked from Georgia and apparently was two hours away from Sioux City.

Karen stated, "We'll pick up Sam no matter where he is."

Unfortunately, Sam had no phone. We hoped someone would share their phone once he grew closer to us.

No call came that Friday night. We prayed for Sam's safety and for God to bless his journey to Washington. He might have walked past Sioux City.

Saturday arrived, and we took Matt and Kimanni to lunch. Matt was a young friend who slept in our loft one sultry summer. We wanted to see him before he left for college.

I barely sat down when the phone rang. My heart leaped with excitement. "It's Sam. He's in Sioux City. I'm going to get him."

Later, as we ate together, I thought about our group. Karen and I had past divorces. Each of these three twenty-year-olds grew up without a steady father presence, some with fathers in prison.

We were all still broken to some degree. At the same time, we could be overcomers, victorious over our pasts.

During those three hours, I listened and laughed. The food was great, but the fellowship was greater. The perfect lunch.

We all gave Matt a hug and wished him well.

We returned home to pack as Karen and I were moving back to Kansas City. Sam stayed to help mow, trim and paint. We ended our daylight at the pool.

As Strange Cats, we had a tradition of tossing a cornhusk at a tree trunk seventy feet off the old wooden back deck. I suggested an age handicap for me but got no sympathy. I threw within three feet of the trunk. "Did you see that throw?" I asked Karen. "They won't beat that. A throw like that deserves a kiss." Karen and I hugged and kissed in front of everybody.

Sam threw a slider, his first attempt missing far right. "I still have one left. I'll do better next time."

Kimanni's final toss landed a foot or so away. My celebration was premature. Kimanni rubbed it in with a humble brag. "I knew I had you."

Sam's final throw hit the trunk. I gave him a high five. "You know what this means. You have to come back next year to defend your crown."

Sunday we went to church and a movie. Neighbor Doug asked if I could help him bale some hay.

Karen brought a camera. Doug's wife, Modine, drove the truck which pulled the trailer. I lifted the heavy square bales to the trailer's edge, then caught a second breath to toss the hay to the next level.

Kimanni and Sam threw to the top with one toss. Doug did some loading and kept the bales in order.

We soon finished, sweating, bonding over our hay bales and looking back over the hill of fresh cut hay. Karen took a picture of us around the bales. Doug and I sat on the back of the trailer for the short ride up the hill.

"That hillside sure is pretty. This has to be one of the prettiest things on earth," he said.

"I like the sweet smell of freshly cut grass. I'm glad you called me to help. It sure was a lot easier with all these young guys."

We closed out the day with a brat and some Iowa sweet corn. We dined and laughed until just past sunset. No one wanted the day to end. It was our last day with Sam.

Our weekend and perfect Saturday lunch here on earth might never happen again. Some things are beyond our control.

So, my dear Father, if it be thy will, I'd like a table for two strange cats and three friends of ours. Please throw in some extra chairs for our friendly neighbors, Doug and Modine. We'd be honored to have you join us along with any other strange cats you bring.

More than a Cabin

In the summer of 2018, Karen and I spent our vacation in the Portland area. Sam assisted his sister in running an outdoor camp at Olympia, Washington. Sam now had a girlfriend, Emily, who worked with them.

The timing was perfect. Sam and Emily met us on their twin tandem bike at Kelso, Washington. Sam wanted us to spend a day and night with him and Emily at his uncle's Tim's cabin built into a steep slope overlooking the Kalama River.

The Kalama River begins at Mount Saint Helen and runs south, ending at the Columbia River. The river runs fast over large boulders left from volcanic activity.

Part of Sam's plan was to treat Karen and me as if we were a king and queen. We were to do nothing. They would feed and entertain us.

They did accept our offer to buy food. We bought all the fixings for a day and morning at the cabin.

We drove to the cabin through the winding two-lane blacktop with its towering pines. I parked at a makeshift dirt clearing. The narrow foot trail led us home.

The cabin was hundreds of feet above the river's floor, yet we could still hear the melodic roar of the crystal-clear river below. From the edge of the cabin's deck we could touch the upper portion of a vibrantly green Douglas Fir.

Scripture speaks of the man who looks in awe at nature and challenges man to deny that there is a God. Even if we have never read the Bible or heard its words, through sight we could be sure God exists. Perhaps the Kalama River is proof of God's existence to all its visitors.

We left the deck for a slow descending walk to the roaring source. Sam reminded me of a college professor teaching about the flora of the Cascades. I stopped to marvel at the beauty of the lush mossy forest, so many flowers intricately woven among edible berries. Sam knew them all.

We reached a boulder large enough for everyone. Sam dove in, the chill of the moment traded for the thrill of the moment. I raced a stick with Karen in the swift current, then skipped some rocks on Kalama's calmer side. Sam and Emily joined in with a stick race of their own.

We returned to the boulder where I noticed a tiny daisy. Its root as small as a needle's thread, somehow it reached upward, unable to topple. A radiant smile added to its blossoming face. The daisy appeared to barely hang on yet was beautiful and strong. A bumblebee drank some nectar and flew away at record speed.

I told Emily, "This flower, what a metaphor for life. Who knows the struggles, the perilous times, the situations where so many of us are just holding on by a thread of hope? No matter where we are or what we've done, we can still share whatever beauty remains in us. We can still live to make the world a better place."

Emily replied, "That's so true."

We returned to the cabin where Sam and Emily's hospitality was evident with the best meal of our trip. The canyon's pines held the scent of grilled steaks, well done. The buttery baked potatoes balanced out the meal that Emily and I topped off with peanut M & M'S. Nevertheless, the best part of the meal was the company.

"We'll do the dishes."

Sam raised his voice politely, "No way. We're here to serve you."

The day found its way to a card game of Railroad Rummy. Sam and Emily were quite competitive, perhaps remnants of Sam's rugby days and Emily's volleyball matches. It was nice to have a day and evening without a TV and cell phones.

Before bedtime, I returned to the deck to marvel at the night sky, the count of heaven above. Sam found the hammock, Emily the couch, and Karen and I, a warm cozy bedroom where we fell asleep to the symphonic river.

The next day I awoke at dawn, greeted by cool crisp air. I sat on one of the deck's chairs and savored every moment. A stellar jay jumped branch to branch on the pine tree. A swallowtail danced in the air. Somewhere, an osprey cried.

Bacon over creamed cheese served in a large green bell pepper was soon served, our hosts repeating yesterday's priceless blessings. I don't know which was best, the bacon's smell or its taste.

Sam and Emily showed us what it was like to be young, in love, and having fun. What joy they seemed to realize from serving. What happiness they brought us.

We were late to our next appointment. Who could blame us?

I read Tim's cabin journal. It was filled with stories of love shared and reflections, confirming that everyone loves his place.

I penned a word of thanks for Tim, Sam, and Emily to read — the day Karen and I became a king and queen, the day we were served by two hospitable souls named Sam and Emily.

My Wife`s Day

Until I became a man, I failed to appreciate my mom. Now married with a wife and four children, I am amazed at what my wife accomplishes each day. It`s not easy to comprehend the beauty of complexity.

She is a wife, a lover, best friend, and mother.

A mom is her child`s best friend whether he knows it or not. She`s the diaper changer, child feeder, teacher, tutor, comforter, nurse, doctor, counselor, cheerleader, and chauffer.

The home is hers. She`s a decorator for all seasons, anniversaries, and birthdays. Her cabinets and refrigerator are full. She cooks dinner and cleans the dishes. Cleaning continues throughout the house with every room attended week after week.

My wife also holds a paying job as a special education teacher. She`s an accountant, a maintenance lady, and a great neighbor.

At church, she sings and helps with Sunday School and prays to comfort and save souls... Away from church, she`s also a prayer warrior.

While wearing so many hats, she remains beautiful within and without, smiling at the world. Who knows what task she will do a minute, hour, or day from now? She wears all her hats well.

As she floats her way from person to person, she showers the world with righteousness and love.

I am grateful for the privilege of her presence in my life.

Some days are a sprint where time goes by too fast. Other moments may seem like a marathon where she can't see the end. My wish is that her roller coaster days always end on a high.

I hope it gives her a small measure of comfort knowing I will help, listen, hug, and love her always.

I will hold the light when things seem dark. In addition, I will help with physical, emotional, and spiritual strength to get us through together.

With God's help we run the race. There is no one on earth I would rather run it with than my wife.

Her love touches everyone.

Father, You and I are pleased with Karen. She is a lover of all just as you are. Give her wisdom and strength as she touches so many lives. Listen to her cries and give her comfort and confidence, for she lives to please all.

Help her to be victorious over sin and when she fails, pick her up gently, forgive graciously. Reassure her that she is capable of that which you require of her.

Help me to understand and to empathize with what she went through today. Give me a proper word or a silent tongue as needed.

I know her love binds the family. Her overflowing fountain of love and righteousness to the world is a great gift.

She is a beautiful woman of integrity, a lover of many and friend of all, a beautiful creation just as she is, growing prettier each day.

We are the fortunate ones blessed by your creation, my Karen, my wife. God, you've done well with her. Thank you.

Amen.

Is it Pleasant Again?

My wife and I live in a town called Pleasant Valley. If only things were always pleasant.

Our neighbor Betty and I both suffered losses this year. My mother passed away in January and Vernon, Betty`s husband of sixty-nine years, died in March.

"Betty`s outside," came the proclamation from our grandson, Owen.

We stared out the window and noticed our neighbor and her daughter standing in their driveway. Something had to be wrong because it was one of those sweltering days where sweat comes without exertion. Why were they outside? We went to find out.

Betty had locked herself out and waited for another daughter to bring a key. I hurried back home to get four cold washcloths to cool everyone off.

Owen joined the conversation, "I'm selling trash bags for our football team. Do you want some?"

Suddenly he had two more customers. I reminded him to thank the women.

Tree limbs from a recent storm littered Betty`s back yard.

Betty said, "They`re too much to manage."

"I'll take care of them tomorrow."

The next day I had new firewood for future evenings of s'mores for the grandchildren.

A few days later, someone knocked on our door. Betty came with two slabs of ribs and a sweet card. Locked away in a past conversation she had listened to a comment I made about my favorite place to buy ribs.

I told Karen, "Let's eat those ribs soon with Betty, then no one will be alone. I can let her know again that I miss her husband. We should never forget our loved ones, and I loved him."

Later that same week Betty attended the Pleasant Valley Senior luncheon. After the Pledge of Allegiance and the Lord's Prayer, Betty said, "Let's send a card or visit those that couldn't make it today. I know how it feels to be alone."

We ate the ribs before Thanksgiving. We shared how we played railroad rummy with Vernon and Betty one time before he passed away.

"Vernon had a twisted smile that brought me laughter," I said. "Our times with the two of you were always good. I miss Vernon. We're here for you."

Before we played railroad rummy, we took the railroad decoration that sat on my mother's ninetieth birthday cake — a reminder of the fun times Mom gave her church friends by introducing them to a new card game. We take the memorial out every time we play.

Is life pleasant again? I think so, but never as pleasant as when Mom and Vernon were with us.

A Lesson from Waverly

My wife and I watched the finale of Vacation Bible School in Waverly, Missouri.

Waverly, Missouri, is a small rural town of 832 according to the most recent census count. My wife and I expected to see our grandchild Owen among a few children with their parents and grandparents in attendance. To our surprise, we met several hundred of them.

We arrived early and managed to secure one of the few remaining parking lot spots. *What was going on with so many cars? Were we at the right place?*

Waverly's churches apparently set aside their doctrines to be one town under God for Vacation Bible School.

The churches created a new dress code. All those attending Vacation Bible School wore tie- dyed t-shirts that read, "When churches unite, God things happen." Rich and poor became equal in everyone's sight.

Children sang songs in unison while the parents joined in.

"There`s Owen," I said. "Do you think he sees us?"

He waved to confirm it.

A father wove through the standing room crowd. His wife just behind him like a running back following her lineman to find their perfect place for the perfect photo.

We enjoyed the event much more than the Royals' game we missed on TV.

Every eye focused on the video of camp. The children became shining stars, something their parents and grandparents already knew.

The participants of camp raised money throughout the week — beyond expectations with a goal exceeded.

When people unite with God, "God things happen."

The citizens united for God as Waverly united for the children. The people stepped up on a weekday and became one nation, under God, with liberty and justice for all. It was a very God thing.

CHAPTER TWO

FALL

I love You. Yes, I Do.

Is it possible to write in six words something more profound and powerful than an epic novel?

Karen and I visited my mother-in-law, Ruth, at the nursing home. Ruth Scofield aka (Lee Scofield) was a published author of a dozen inspirational romance books. I decided to read one of her books.

Karen asked, "What did you think?"

"Wow! She's really talented." I ended up reading several of her books.

She no longer writes those long historic novels or takes trips to the library or historical sites to bring life to her characters. Two strokes and dementia have taken away her mobility along with the ability to write long engaging novels. At one point a doctor got Hospice involved as he thought she was dying. She overcame death and wrote what could arguably be the most profound words she ever penned which she left with us on our last visit with her.

Ruth finds it entertaining to color. Perhaps in her own way, she gets lost in the joy of creation just as she did in childhood. Occasionally she pencils a sketch, usually of Charles, her deceased husband of 54 years.

As I watched her reach for a color, I noticed a sketch she had done in pencil. The plain white paper showed a woman and on the other side, a man — the married couple, Charles and Ruth.

With her mental and physical capacities, this was a great piece of art. But something was added that made it a masterpiece. From the top of the page to the bottom, between the faces, were six words repeated over and over, six words we all long to hear, "I love you. Yes, I do".

Her words these days are few, usually somewhat in a pattern. Always, "Where's Karen? She`s been gone a long time."

Then upon Karen`s return, "What took you so long?"

On today`s visit Mom said, "Kiss me," her sense of love and touch still evident.

The visit was over quickly. I gently placed my hand on her shoulder and softly kissed her on the cheek. As I left with her last chapter in hand, I repeated those same words she shared earlier, "I love you. Yes, I do."

Labor Day at the Dell

What makes a great weekend? Is it the place, the events, or the people?

Karen and I looked forward to a Labor Day weekend for a reprieve from forty-five-hour work weeks. We continued the tradition of inviting Terry and his crew from Omaha, along with his grandson, Caleb, who was ten.

My daughter Alicia brought her three-year-old son Owen from Kansas City.

Our bungalow was a modest three bedrooms with a basement, finished like a lodge. A built-in aquarium perched in the corner. Above the aquarium was a window well where toads thrived and made us feel as if we lived at the zoo.

Our surroundings included a garden, pool, aesthetic pond, fire pit and a trail through an acre of woods. Across the dead-end gravel road was the neighbor's pond where permission to fish was secured.

Prior to Alicia's arrival, Owen asked that time tested question, "Are we there yet?"

"Just two more episodes of Paw Patrol," was my daughter's response.

As soon as Caleb arrived, he cornered me with a litany of questions. Can we walk the trail? Can we have a fire?"

"You'll have to ask your mother or your grandparents."

I secretly hoped they would say yes to all his questions. I was anxious for a weekend tour of service, to share the gift of hospitality along with my beautiful wife.

Karen and I often pray that those visiting us feel rested and relaxed while having fun.

They loved the four-foot pool. Even Owen despite his three- foot frame. Which was more fun, the splash or the laugh that followed?

The garden gave a harvest of fresh lettuce. broccoli, beans, and tomatoes. The forest kicked in with some venison steaks. Our grill filled the air with the aroma of one last summer barbecue.

I spoke my usual nervous prayer. Praying in public is not my thing. Owen showed us all how to end with a boisterous, "Amen, Amen, Amen."

We ate quickly so as not to ignore the pond with gifts of large blue gill and bass. Oh, how I wished the trip could last. The setting sun cast a shadow on the calm waters and told us it was time for a campfire.

The s'mores though messy, tasted delicious. We licked our fingers, leaving table manners behind. A drop of rain with an interrupting crash of thunder ushered us back to the bungalow.

Karen spoke to her helper, Caleb. "Isn't lightning awesome? Did you hear the thunder? That's God's fireworks in the sky."

I love my wife's heart. She makes me proud to be her husband.

We replaced the campfire with a game of hand and foot. During the card game, I stretched my foot under the table and found the arch of Karen's foot. Her blue eyes twinkled, and she followed with a flirtatious smile, the one she has repeated since I have known her, the one that says I love you, yes, I still love you. Though we've shared this touch a good fifteen years, it never grows old.

Our day of fun in the sun wore out some of the older bodies, so we didn't finish the game.

We opened the screen door and gave the frogs of the aesthetic pond their moment to sing. The gentle rain joined with a soothing sound. Maybe the frogs were giving thanks knowing their home would be secure with another summer rain. Maybe the rain just wanted to see how they sounded together.

I snuggled close to Karen's warm body, silently giving thanks for her and our day at the dell. The harmonious sounds of the night put us quickly to sleep. We awoke for breakfast, the great weekend nearly over.

Caleb asked, "Can we come back next year?"

"We hope so. You'll need to check with your mom."

Hugs held back tears just before they drove away.

Alicia left later that afternoon. "We'll see you at Thanksgiving or Christmas."

What is the answer for a great weekend, the place, the event, or the people? We all must choose for ourselves.

For me, it's the people. Our weekend together confirmed that family is fun, love is binding, and joy comes from giving. Karen and I gave love and took back the gifts happiness gave through Godly fellowship.

Don`t Ask about the Squirrels

Karen and I vacationed several days in the Black Hills of South Dakota, but we never saw a squirrel. I see squirrels everywhere I go. Why are there no squirrels in the Black Hills?

Before going to Spearfish Canyon, we stopped to visit Mother Nature at the local gas station. Before entering, I told Karen I was going to find out why there are no squirrels in the Black Hills.

At the counter stood a young female clerk and two elderly men about to check out. I took them to be locals.

"How come there are no squirrels in the Black Hills?"

One of the men gave me the you-shouldn`t-have-asked-that-question look

"Are you serious? I've already shot 29 squirrels and still have three to go. They cause a lot of damage to my home."

Was his face red because he was angry? I should have never asked the question. My inquiry turned to fear.

Then the buddy chimed in, "He thinks he`s funny. You shouldn`t joke around like that. I went to sit in my truck one day and noticed a lump in my seat. Those little varmints had taken the foam right out of my seat. They stored their pinecones underneath. You ever sat on pinecones?

"'I`m sorry. No, I haven`t."

"Well, they're sharp. They went right through that seat into my rear."

I quickly looked towards the ladies' room and the front exit. Thank God, Karen was there.

"Are you ready to go? Are you okay?"

"Let`s go."

Security replaced manners. I felt safe in the car and explained the story to Karen.

As we left, I saw a squirrel. He ran with a pinecone in his mouth, headed for that fellow's pickup truck. I watched him go under the hood, but never saw him come out.

Still Wounded

Karen and I wanted to take in some history, so we decided to drive to Wounded Knee. We read multiple accounts of the last battle between the Lakota and the United States Army. Thirty-one of the army men died. The Native American casualties were over 300 and included woman and children.

Men from the army received Medals of Honor. The Lakotas lie in a small burial site.

What honor is there in killing a woman or a child? What`s been done to right the wrong?

After visiting Mount Rushmore and Crazy Horse, we were returning home. We envisioned a well-maintained memorial site but discovered nothing more than a few dollars were raised to honor their loved ones. The site revealed only a couple parking spaces and a sign that led us to a trail to the unkempt cemetery atop a nearby hill.

I dodged the ruts leading up the hill.

The cemetery was depressing as a Native American man shared the life history of those buried. Some, if not all, were exploited by the white man.

I left silent, wanting to ask questions but feeling a greater need to pay my respects, to listen and reflect on the sad terrifying words. "She was running away with her child in her arms, unarmed, when a soldier shot them both."

After just a few stories, we had heard enough. We felt sick and depressed.

Wounded Knee left me with the feeling of injustice, a battle fought unfairly. The cavalry owned the repeating firearms and the cannon, while the Indians used single shot weapons.

The Indians fought men. The cavalry fought fleeing women and children along with their men.

The Indians once populated the Black Hills, when gold was discovered, the white man took the land.

Those Native Americans were no different from me. They wanted the best for their families. In their culture perhaps, a beautiful fertile land where buffalo roamed. The land at Wounded Knee appeared rocky and hilly without a fertile crop. No buffalo.

"I'm sorry for how we treated you."

The memorial site is a mourning site, one we all should see to realize the injustice. The Lakota will always be, still wounded at Wounded Knee.

Sammy the Cat

She loves me not. She loves me.

While growing up, I never had a cat. My life changed when Karen found Sammy at Royal Family Kids Camp. Sammy was primarily an outside cat.

Karen called her our mouser. Sammy often chose to sleep on the shelves of our Morton garage. When she came in, she was all Karen's.

My relationship with Sammy was one of unaffectionate mutual respect. She ate mice in the barn. I lived inside where I ate meat and potatoes. We were both fine with the arrangement.

All this was about to change. We were moving to Kansas City, and Karen moved first.

I became Sammy's master. She treated me as her disaster. Since Sammy was becoming a house cat, she needed declawed. Sammy felt I needed clawed.

As I tried to put her into the cat carrier, all claws were on kennel. They flailed in all directions, drawing blood.

"Sammy, you know, this makes us blood sisters, brothers, something?"

Apparently, I wasn't funny. I heard no meow, just a hiss. Getting her out would be easier. Rough grey gloves covered my hands while making the exchange at the vet.

I managed to avoid a fight. "Don't mind the carrier. I'll pick it up when I return to get her."

Since her demeanor was angry, I didn't mind our few days apart while she recovered at the clinic. Despite everything, I still wished Sammy a continued recovery to keep Karen happy.

We headed home. Again, no meow. "I'm glad you're coming home, Sammy."

Her hazel eyes pierced my soul or maybe it was cat intuition. Sammy knew Karen wasn't around and she wasn't about to give me her time of day.

When we returned home, there was still rage in the cage. That hiss returned. I showed Sammy my gloves and opened the door. She ran as fast as she could to the barn. I sensed she felt imprisoned, abused, used by me, but at least she was able to get free and run for her life. At least this time, I was unharmed.

I didn't see her for days. At least I could tell Karen the food and water was disappearing. Sammy likely ate in the dead of night when I couldn't see her.

I bet Garfield wouldn't treat me like this.

There is a time to heal, a time to mourn, a time to forgive, and a time to love. Maybe there is also a time to be left alone.

Maybe that time was now.

I worked and packed boxes. Life had put our relationship into neutral if not reverse, but soon things would slowly change as I gave Sammy time to mourn.

I began to see her at a distance, whining, pining for Karen. Sammy finally came closer and acknowledged me while brushing me away. I reached down to hug her, but she ran to the barn. She wasn't ready to be with me.

"We'll be moving soon, Sammy, and you'll see Karen." These words of hope seemed to make a difference, as I was able to touch her again — without gloves.

We completed our move, and I worked from home ten hours a day. Karen arrived home in the late afternoon. Sammy had a new home with us. She was happy.

One day I sat in my pajamas and soft warm socks. With a rattling purr, Sammy brushed up against my feet.

Now I often find her nestled under my desk atop my toes that are her pillow. Day after day, Sammy is my companion. When I get up, she follows me. Sammy trusts me.

After I finish work, I often sit in the recliner. She jumps into my arms and we touch and touch again. I talk to her and she purrs contentedly.

She loves me not. No, she loves me.

Love Routines

Alicia called. "You know I have that new job in Kansas City. I want to be sure I'm acclimated with the new work. Could you guys take Owen for a week?" Owen was three years old.

"That should be fine. Let me check with Karen."

"Hey Karen, where should Owen sleep? You think he should sleep with us?"

"I`ve already thought of that. We`ll get the air mattress out. We`ll put him in your office. That way he`ll be close to us."

Every night, I heard these words, "Grandma, could you read a book?"

"You bet I can."

After a couple days of the reading routine, Owen came to my office with a stack of books. "Where`s Karen?" The love routine had caught on.

Every morning when Owen woke up, he said the same thing, "Mom?"

"Grandpa`s here. Mom's still at work. In four more days, she'll come to get you."

Owen grabbed "Blankie," his grey security blanket, the perfect size for his three-foot frame. He wrapped the blanket tightly around his body and staggered into my arms.

No words are exchanged. His legs fell onto my lap. His head slouched to my left shoulder. I hugged him, a long hug that turned into a warm soft snuggle.

When I sensed he could hear me, I repeated the same words I said every day, "Owen, I love you."

"I love you too."

What's a love routine? Owen has shown us. Find the one you love and call out their name. If they're not at home, find Grandma and Grandpa. Hug a little, snuggle a little, and always say, "I love you."

In the giving of that love, we discover we too are loved.

Potato Patch Lessons

What can we learn from a Potato Patch?

My grandchild refers to my neighbor as Farmer Doug. This farmer has years of potato- growing experience with rows stretching a hundred yards.

"Hey Doug, can you help me plant five rows of potatoes at the top of our hill? The space is only ten by twenty yards. That will leave space to plant a few pumpkins."

"`I`d be glad to help."

"We`ll plow some rows." Doug brought his friend, John Deere.

"What do we do with these potatoes you gave us?"

"Cut them in halves. Be sure each section has at least two buds. Then plant each section one foot apart. You should water them after planting."

Our hose wouldn`t stretch that far.

"When do we pick them?"

"When the foliage on the potatoes dies. Wait two weeks and you'll discover life below."

I imagined mashed potatoes, fries, baked potatoes, and potatoes to devour with eggs. Several months later Doug and I talked again.

"How are the potatoes coming?"

"I think they're ready to dig up."

"Good, we can test out my new digger."

I politely declined. Digging the eight inches into the dirt would be a way to exercise and shed a pound or two. I also wanted a small crew to help me dig.

Doug frowned. "If you change your mind, let me know."

I arranged for Kimanni's sixteen-year-old brother Herbie to join us along with eleven-year- old Matthew. They were both from fatherless homes.

"Now guys, you see this dead foliage. Potatoes could be directly below, so be sure you put the shovel to the side a bit so you don't slice through them. We can eat baked potatoes with dinner."

Matthew knew what he was doing. He dug enough potatoes to feed us for a week. "Look how big this one is."

Herbie was not to be outdone. "Check out the size of this one. Can we get a picture?"

Karen joined us. "Hold your potato off to the side of your body. That's good." She checked her phone. "I'll send the pictures to your moms."

Was it fun for them or did they just like work? Maybe it was the company. Perhaps they felt important with a picture taken. It may have been everything.

The smell of grilled venison filled the deck's air to go with our freshly baked potatoes topped with melted butter.

"Boys, how'd you like the meal?"

Herbie spoke, "Great."

Matthew added, "Those potatoes were the best."

"Guys, I think we picked them at just the right time. Thanks for your help."

Herbie added final words. "When I grow up, I'm going to have a potato patch."

The next day Karen and I walked along the woodsy trail that led to the potato patch. The walk with my best friend was peaceful and left me with moments to cherish.

I took a shovel along. At fifty-eight, one does not harvest five rows of potatoes in a day, so I was ready to dig for more.

Owen joined us the following day. I grabbed the smallest shovel I could find as Owen was just weeks away from his third birthday. The army shovel towered a bit over his head, but he took it from me. Owen seemed determined to carry the shovel to the top of the hill. He finally stumbled and fell from his burden, but without tears. Much to his dismay, I carried the shovel the rest of the way.

Owen watched carefully as I dug up a potato. Then he grabbed the shovel. He jumped on it, but his effort was as if digging into concrete. I turned the earth loose. He took to all fours, grabbed the shovel from me, and placed his tiny hands into the dirt. Owen placed the clods on the shovel, stood tall and flung them away.

The potato patch and its crew shared a lesson or two:
- Seek wise council and grow.
- A faithful neighbor starts and finishes a job.
- It's more fun when we share.
- Don't always pick up a child when they fall.
- Sometimes we learn by failures. Keep digging.
- Be there when someone needs help.
- Children, even teenagers, want undivided attention.
- Children follow our behaviors.
- A potato patch is more than potatoes.
- A freshly baked potato with melted butter tastes the best.

Every time I eat potatoes, I'm reminded of happy times with my neighbor and the harvesting crew from the potato patch.

The Last Pumpkin

Atop our hill sat the little pumpkin, trying to grow past the first frost. It managed to reach four inches wide, two inches tall, orange, ready for harvest.

"Owen, Let`s pick a pumpkin. Do you want to go?"

"Ya," came the excited reply.

We left immediately for the garden adjacent to the potato patch. "Can you see it, Owen? There it is, right there under those weeds. Pull, you can do it. Harder, pull, harder and use both hands."

He tugged and tugged. The weeds had a chokehold around the stem. One final tug and he pulled the pumpkin, weeds and all, before he fell on his behind. "I`m okay."

He pulled the weeds free and held up his trophy. "I did it, Grand-pa. I did it."

"Great job, Owen. I knew you could do it."

He wanted to tell everyone and off he ran, but not far. His right foot turned in the potato hole and he fell.

"Oh no, it hurts." He sat and rubbed his temporary ankle pain away.

Down the hill heading for Grandma, his long stride got the best of him and he fell again, but still held the pumpkin.

Oh my gosh! "Are you okay?"

"I`m okay. Grandma, I picked the pumpkin. See?"

"Oh, that`s a nice pumpkin."

"I did it, Grandma. It was hard, but I pulled harder and harder liked Grandpa said. The weeds had it, but I l got it. I got it myself."

"You did a great job."

Owen ran to the side door. "Momma, Momma, I got the pumpkin. It`s for you."

She bowed down to him and embraced him with a big hug. "Owen, you`re so sweet. We`ll have to put it somewhere so everyone can see it. I`m proud of you."

Owen was happy. Little boys are no different from grown men. They get their thrill from the acknowledgement of their work.

That evening while eating mashed potatoes, I noticed a beautiful orange centerpiece. "Where did that come from?"

"I picked it. Can we pick pumpkins next year?"

"Yes, yes we can."

After the meal was finished, I paraphrased the story to Owen with final thoughts. "In the falls of life, always get up. Run to all those who love you. Someday when you have a child of your own, pick a pumpkin with him or her. They`ll never forget it."

The Words of Yesterday

This is the worst day ever.

I grabbed Ian`s iPad and insisted that he join the rest of us to rake leaves. "You`re going with us. You can play with that later. It`s a beautiful day and we`re going to rake some leaves and jump into them. You`re not going to ruin the fun we`re all going to have."

I envisioned a day long ago where I threw my son into a pile of leaves. The photos showed him smiling. I still remembered his request, "Do it again."

Karen overheard what I said to Ian and came to support me. "Ian, Grandma and Grandpa are going to give you a penny for every stick you pick up."

Ian replied, "I`m not playing."

Karen responded, "That's fine, but you`ll still go outside with us."

Ian`s sister Heidi was more receptive, taking the challenge as an adventure. But as soon as she saw nuts on the ground, she became distracted. "These nuts are looking at us."

I responded, "Those are buckeyes."

"Can we get a bucket so I can keep them?"

It wasn't long before the bucket was full. "Are there other nuts here?"

I quickly found another pail. Heidi filled the bucket with walnuts, acorns, hickory nuts, pecans, and a few leaves of red and yellow. She even managed to cram in a couple of sticks.

Owen found a wheelbarrow. With the penny-for-every-stick reward, he was on a focused mission to become rich. He filled the wheelbarrow with large and small sticks and won with a total of sixty-one.

"I got the most. I got sixty-one."

Guess we must work on humility.

Ian hung around to watch Grandpa rake leaves. Soon he grabbed another rake and worked on his own pile. He jumped right in. The two of us combined and formed a large pyramid of leaves. I grabbed him and threw him in.

Then I heard the words of yesterday. "Do it again."

I called to Karen, "Can you get some pictures?"

I took the other two kids and tossed them high above autumn's mattress. They landed in leafy delight. Smiles. Laughter. Then they repeated the delightful words, "Do it again."

They took the sticks to the creek at the back of our property and made them into fishing rods. The orange and red leaves on the creek became fish. Owen grabbed the fish, counting each as if he were in the next contest.

Ian grabbed a long branch and joined in. "I caught one. It's yellow. It's a sunfish."

The next month when they visited, the first one out the backdoor was Ian. Running, playing, having fun.

What can we learn from grandkids and sticks? Maybe that depends on the kids.

Ian learned we could have fun, even on the worst day. Heidi knew there was more to life than sticks. Enjoy it. Owen worked hard because work pays. Once work was over, we smiled and laughed.

The words of my son and now my grandchildren still whisper happily in my ears. "Do it again."

One equals Four

Our washer died, but good came from its passing. Blessings flowed through acts of kindness.

My son Tom and his wife Chelsea did not know about our dilemma, and they were selling their home. Tom asked, "Do you know anyone who needs a washer and dryer?"

We now had upgrades. Kindness blessed us again, but there was still a problem.

How could I move those mammoth machines?

I called our nephew and his friend. These younger men were stronger and up to the task. They seemed excited about moving the machines free of cost. I paid them a bit, as a kind deed deserves a kind act.

The kind deed expanded itself when we learned our niece's family could use a dryer. We gave them our dryer — free.

Blessings did not end there. We learned our young movers could take our damaged washer to a friend. He would sell the machine for scrap.

When our son offered his appliances, when our nephew and his friend helped, when Karen and I gave our dryer, we were all showed kindness. Even the scrap man sold our washer for a profit.

One act of kindness brought four blessings.

One Request

Karen and I attended church in Portland, Oregon.

"Good morning. I don`t believe I know you." Dennis smiled and shook our hands.

"This is my wife, Karen. I`m Tom."

Dennis stood tall in his suit and appeared to be pushing seventy. "How`d you find us?"

"A flyer on a restaurant door referenced a fourth of July tribute. We like to honor those who fight for freedom."

Dennis stared more intently. "I fought in Vietnam. A bomb exploded. I was standing beside my friend who was closer than a brother."

He took a short breath, paused a second, then spoke again in a trembling whisper. "I couldn`t even recognize him. Pray for me."

"Thank you for your service."

Dennis leaned in and lowered his head as if trying to penetrate my soul. "Remember me in your prayers."

"We`ll pray for you and ask others to pray for you as well."

Sometimes words of appreciation are not enough to heal the remaining pain.

Father God forgive us for the sin that leads to war. I don`t know Dennis well, but you do. Give him abundant love, comfort, and peace as he mourns. Please make it known to him that we do pray for him, his fallen brother, and their families.

We thank you for them. We honor them. We love them. We mourn with them. You know their every need. Please provide for them and protect them until they find their peace and rest in you. Amen.

A Walk on Glory Trail

Our grandson Owen was with us for the Thanksgiving holiday. We took a walk along Glory Trail — a small woodsy path lined with reminders of scripture, a place to reflect on God`s word.

The journey`s descent started past a few pine trees. Owen paused and said, "We`ll cut this one." Christmas was coming soon.

"We can`t cut it. It`s too big."

He looked to his left and said, "We'll cut this one."

"It`s also too big."

He gave a dejected look. "We`ll cut a small one." But there were no smaller ones.

We traversed slightly down the hill, then back up again, Owen approached each stepping-stone enthusiastically. "Jump," he repeated. "Jump," stone after stone.

A man`s step is like a child`s jump. With a lot of trouble between life`s stones, sometimes we fail to reach milestones and safe places to land. It sure is easier with proper strength and direction.

As Owen led the way up the trail, I was curious about the journey ahead. He remembered the direction taught earlier in life.

We circled the rectangle of woods back to the part of the yard he played in as a younger child. Owen ran to the sandbox. Plastic tools waited in a corner. "I'll fill the bucket with sand."

The bucket cracked from a frigid winter as I had left it out in the elements. "I'm sorry, Owen."

"It's okay." Even at four, he forgave me quickly. If only we older ones followed Owen's example. He found a new pail but had no plastic shovel. He used a Frisbee as his scoop, filled the bucket with sand. His mission was over.

Owen took the bucket of sand to go show his mother his work. I wished the walk to the sandbox could continue so that I could again relish our time together.

I believe we should all take walks with others. I went on the walk expecting nothing but received everything I needed for that day. I found the joy of a moment and the hope of our future from a child of four. Both were good.

Thanksgiving Fire Men

What`s the best way to prepare for a fire?

At Thanksgiving, the men decided to have a fire off our back deck while the women watched.

The women talked and maintained a safe distance. Children waited anxiously for flames to start so they could ignite a marshmallow or two while trying to cook the perfect s'mores.

Each man had his own way of sizing up the wood. One young man flexed his muscles with a thick stick. Tried to break it. Nothing happened. He hoped the crowd was looking the other way as he grabbed a smaller branch and snapped it in half.

The bended-knee man pulled the limb into his strong knee. He looked for a crack in the wood and listened for a snapping sound. Embarrassment ruled as the limb won. He walked away with head low and searched for a weaker stick.

The baseball bat swing was next. He swung the wood fiercely into the tree trunk. Half the wood went flying while the rest remained in his hands. Fortunately, the other half missed hitting someone.

The next batter took his swing. Nothing happened to the branch but the batter's hands were numb. The next swing was faster with the same result. He optioned for a rotten piece of wood that shattered with his third attempt.

The athletic type tried the jump and snap. Two hands held the limb low. He leaped high but landed from resistance as the wood refused to break. He tried again, this time stumbling and taking a noticed fall. Persistence prevailed when he changed his style and broke the limb over his knee.

The wiser opted for a saw. Even the saw struggled against the hard wood. My son fractured off the end of the saw blade. He eventually prevailed; the wounded saw victorious over the hardwood.

As the men took their turns, they glanced at the children to make sure they were safe. The fire began, and one lad ignited a marshmallow. "Look, I started a fire."

Dad came to the rescue dousing the flame, tearing off the black crust. He gave the luscious center to his son.

Then he taught his son how to cook two at once. One for Mom while the son kept the other.

Dad took the marshmallow to his wife.

"Thank you. I love how you're teaching our son to become a man."

He felt appreciated. Fire men are strongest when they hear the affirming voice of a nurturing woman.

A Man of GOD

When I heard the news of Mic's passing, I cried. Tears came again this morning. Jesus wept. Karen and I wept for his family's loss.

Several comments on social media marked the passing of Mic. Some repeated the cliché, *"Words can`t express."*

Others wrote compassionate words such as, "Sorry. My heart hurts. I have a heavy heart. My head is hung low and I have tears."

Many expressed thoughts about strength, comfort, peace, love, hugs, healing, and prayers.

Others used descriptive words for Mic such as: "Amazing, consistent, encouraging, nice, wonderful and wise."

People used short phrases describing Mic as a "Guitar player, installer of heating and air conditioning equipment, a man of prayer and a man of God."

Some called him, "Mentor, leader, father, friend, husband, worshiper and world changer." Mic was also the church, a servant of God for days other than Sunday.

I first met Mic when I assisted him in teaching a Royal Rangers class. He became my mentor.

Mic and I were golfing friends. In 2014, we won first place at the Convoy of Hope 2014 Golf Tournament. On another occasion, we won first place 2nd flight of the 18th annual RMS Golf Outing.

When I left Sioux City, I golfed one more time with Mic, Pastor Kevin, and Mic`s father, Don. Each of them signed the scorecard as a reminder of the good times we shared.

After Karen and I moved to Kansas City, Mic and Janell became our long-distance friends. We furnished them a place to stay when they traveled to Springfield, Missouri. The last trip was a vivid reminder.

I had recently joined a golf club, so I took Mic golfing. Since I was new to the club, I usually golfed alone. Mic said, "I`m going to pray you have someone to golf with."

Now, every Monday and Tuesday a group of men play golf with me.

Mic gave me a mounting kit for my turkey fans. He and Janell suggested we stay with them on our next trip north. They lived out giving gifts and sharing hospitality.

Mic was a shining example of who we can be, a giver of time, talent, and treasure to God`s glory.

Among a phrase, a photograph, a scorecard, a trophy, and a gift, the greatest gift Mic gave me was when he prayed for me.

One year, I invited Mic and his family for a fishing trip at my neighbor`s pond. I prayed for great weather and an abundant fishing trip.

The day was sunny, and the fish were hungry. No surprise about the fellowship and fun.

One of Mic`s three daughters exclaimed, "Daddy, Daddy, I caught a fish."

Mic reached quickly for the camera.

Later the same child shouted, "Daddy, Daddy, I caught another fish."

After we finished, she told her mom about what fun she had with her daddy. "Mommy, Mommy, I caught twenty fish."

The Bible talks about fishing for men and being a man of God. Based on the responses I read after Mic's passing, he had a whole congregation of followers: men, women, and children.

Mic could now tell God the Father, "Daddy, Daddy, I caught a fish."

Jesus once asked, "Who do you say I am?"

If someone asked me the same question about Mic, I would answer, "He is a man of God."

Chapter Three

Winter

Switchgrass Restored

In early December we witnessed our first Iowa storm. A gentle rain fell. Quickly, it turned to freezing rain, then a heavy wet snow.

The next morning the five-foot high switchgrass near our aesthetic pond was bowled over by the weight of winter. It lay flat on the ground. I shook a heavy blade free of snow and ice, then held up the grass. When I let go, it fell. Was it dead or beyond repair?

I went to the shed for a sickle to even out the grass since it was not lying uniform. A brisk wind convinced me to start the job tomorrow.

It reminded me of a parent wanting to rescue an adult child. As a life burden overcomes the child, the parent tries to hold him up only to see him fall. Nothing works. The parent prays for someone else to help the child.

Sunshine made an entrance mid-morning. Something beyond my explanation occurred. The grass now stood at attention in the afternoon light. Was the grass reaching for the sun? Did the sun melt away yester-day's burden?

Whenever I observe nature mingled with life, I am humbled by all I don't know.

Those tall grass moments of life form who we are, what hope we have and what we believe.

I believe God is in control. If God can restore the switchgrass to stand tall again, how much more might he do for you and me?

Do Tattoos Speak?

At Casey`s gas station, I greeted the worker, "Good morning. How are you doing?"

The clerk quickly approached the counter. His hair was thick and black with a coal-black beard. His tan was a deep brown. He wore quarter sized solid black earrings. Despite the morning frost, he wore a short-sleeved shirt. A fat tattooed yellow duck nestled on his left arm with an unidentified symbol of three black dots on his right forearm.

"That will be a dollar ninety-nine."

"If you don`t mind me asking, what`s up with your tattoos?"

He looked at me with lips pressing in, not saying a thing.

I tried to make myself clearer. "What do they mean? You don`t have to answer unless you want to."

He leaned over the counter, looked into my eyes, and pointed toward the duck. "This one reminds me of my stillborn son."

Suddenly, my preconceived ideas melted away as we shared commonality. I lost a child in the first trimester.

"I`m sorry."

I waited forever for his response. No answer, only silence.

"What's the other one for?"

He pointed to the top of his forearm and indicated, "This one's a symbol for hope. He turned his arm over, "This one's for faith."

"Thank you for telling me your story." The tattoos spoke silently, softly to my soul. He honored his son and displayed words that got him through each day.

I'm not sure I have the emotional strength to wear a reminder of my departed son so visibly, day after day, month after month, year after year. In my reality and perhaps his, the tattoos are timeless words spoken in art.

I'll see you today
I'll see you tomorrow
I'll see you forever

I'll not forget the past
You live in the present
Forever you will last.

They can't take my faith
They can't take my hope
They can't take my love.

I never asked the clerk his name, but he left a lasting impression.

We can all do better not to judge a man before hearing him. But we cannot hear unless we ask and try to understand what makes us different or what unites us.

Watching his grieving eyes, I heard his compassionate voice and felt the timeless love and pride of a father for his child.

Yes, tattoos speak.

An Icy Day

A deceiving landscape crept over the dell's hill as if life were secure and beautiful. The sun illuminated each tree, adorned heavily in shimmering icy makeup . Beyond the beauty, each bore winter's weight. The trees limbs tried to survive without a collapse, destroying itself or someone else.

The sun shone only for a minute. The sky turned grey.

The icy weight flattened the ornamental tall grass to the dell's floor.

The north wind blew the chimes. A bird sang his refrain, perhaps a warning of things to come. A closer look revealed a bright red cardinal singing to his camouflaged mate. Maybe a happier song for times ahead.

Ice sickles fought gravity and stretched from the gutters toward the ground. The front sidewalk was frozen. The back deck covered with ice, required a cautious step. I exited the back door with a hand on the rail and held a bag of cracked corn to spread across the yard.

Brown sparrows joined the cardinals for breakfast. Morning fox squirrels rested in a hollow tree.

The teacher slept in, waiting for a safer day. The wood I gathered earlier filled the fireplace with golden flames. Karen awakened to a cup of warm fragrant tea at the breakfast table. Soon she sat at the piano and played classic tunes.

I paused to take a work break. What was most beautiful: the fire, the piano, or my wife?

My wife, of course, with a tie for second.

The hours passed quickly. Karen made a cup of hot tomato soup to go with grilled-cheese sandwiches.

I returned to my work window and noticed a flock of turkeys.

The afternoon was nearly over.

A whitetail doe and her fawn arrived for an early dinner.

I finished the day, turned off my computer, and returned to the fireplace to make sure the fire remained strong.

Karen called out, "Dinner is ready."

I reached for her hand and we gave thanks that we were safe and warm on an icy day.

Ten Gifts from Three

I was proud of Alicia for the qualities she instilled in Owen.
Alicia, "Please don`t let Owen spend anything on me for Christmas because I've already received ten gifts from him

1. **Kisses** What says love more than a kiss?

2. **Hugs** Who doesn`t want to hug a child back for his unconditional love?

3. **I love you** He says it so often and reminds us all to do the same.

4. **Clinging** I hold him upside down and tickle his tummy or drag him along as he tugs at my leg laughing all the way. The gift includes security, love, laughter, and fun.

5. **Proclamation** Owen says, "I love church." These words soothe my soul.

6. **Relationship** Owen calls out, "Where`s honey?" My nickname for my wife. Owen knows a good mentor when he meets one.

7. **Enthusiasm** He brings joy with words, "Ho, Ho, Ho."

8. **Service** He helps arrange Grandpa's pills into his daily pill container.

9. **Time** Owen takes time for the morning hug and kiss along with the evening hug and kiss.

10. **Thank You** He knows the sacrifices his mom makes and recognizes them with his "Thank you."

This Christmas I will receive gifts that will not last but the gifts from Owen and lessons taught by Alicia are priceless gifts for all seasons.

The Heart of Christmas

After Christmas shopping, Owen and I returned to our car. We met the heart of Christmas.

"Sir," a woman's pleading voice from a car parked across from us.

Her vehicle was parked diagonally in a horizontal handicap spot. The rear passenger door was open. She leaned toward the back seat. Her snowy white hair and her pace indicated an elderly woman.

Was she hurt? Why was she bent over?

Sensing the worst, I hurried to help her. Her right hip and arm turned and stretched to reach something.

She turned toward us with her head bent down and handed Owen an orange Fuzzy Puppy toy.

"Owen, tell her thank you."

"Thank you."

No response from the woman.

What should I say? An awkward shoulder hug stole time to find words. "Merry Christmas ma`am. Thank you. You`re so kind."

She remained silent. Tears welled up in the corner of my eyes as I walked away.

Curiosity made me wonder how many stuffed animals she gave away. Did we get the last one? Did we get the only one?

I drove across the lot, then circled back to talk to her again. Her car was empty.

She headed to the store with shuffling feet marching in unison with her husband's slow cadence. They held hands as if holding one another up. He opened the door slowly as I watched her grand exit out of my life.

My part was a helping hand. Hers was a giving hand. Owen's was a loving hand. He already had a new name for Fuzzy Puppy.

"This is Lulu. She likes oranges. That's why she's orange. Take good care of her when I'm gone with Mom."

That day we saw giving, kindness, and love as the heart of Christmas brought joy to a child.

Don`t Change a Thing

People like to refer to the good old days as if they were somehow better than present times.

One Christmas, I took my wife and ten-year-old Kimanni to see *It`s a Wonderful Life*. It was the first time Kimanni had seen the movie.

Sioux City`s Orpheum was restored to the beauty of youth at the cost of roughly twelve million dollars. The soft red seats reclined so we could see the sparkling chandelier hanging from the ceiling.

After the film, Kimanni beamed like the chandelier. "That was great. I know what we`ll do next year. We`ll see this movie again. It`s a tradition."

I never realized how much impact one night could have on a child's life. My heart swelled with joy.

Life took us away from the Orpheum. Recently, our grandson Owen confirmed it was a wonderful life in a different way.

The aroma of freshly baked bread greeted us at the Pizza Hut door. The thought of supreme pizza made my mouth water.

As we waited for our order, I asked Owen. "Is there anything you would change about Grandma and Grandpa?"

Owen hugged Grandma and said, "You`re the best!"

"What about Grandpa? Is there anything you would change about Grandpa?"

"Nothing."

I was elated by Owen's responses. Maybe as grandparents, we were doing something right.

In our imperfect world, for one night in the past and one day in the present Karen and I felt as if we were somewhere between Cloud Nine and Heaven.

Maybe next year we'll take Owen and Kimanni to the movie, then close out the night at Pizza Hut.

I Want to Go Home

People in nursing homes often say, "I want to go home." At Christmas time, they say it more often.

Karen and I entered the commons area to visit her eighty-four-year-old mother, Ruth.

Three other residents slightly lifted their heads. Their sparkling eyes enlarged with raised eyebrows. Half-smiles appeared. No complete smiles left to give.

Gary caught my eye. His Forest Gump posture accentuated his slender six-foot frame. His voice was a mumbling whisper.

"How are you, Gary?" I asked. He gave me an up-and-down nod.

The attendant told me Gary had no visitors. He was homeless. He accepted a cold six-pack of Coke I gave him. His nod thanked me.

Gary usually sat with Jerry whose memory had faded along with his eyesight.

"I`m from Nebraska. I need to get back home."

"Where do you live, Jerry?"

He paused ten seconds. "I don`t…I can`t remember. It`s somewhere around Omaha."

"I know you like to read. I brought you this magnifying glass so you can see the letters."

No thankfulness. Just half smiles and a nod.

I moved toward Ruth. Gary sipped his Coke and gave the others to his friends. Jerry moved his present closer to the newspaper. He never let go of the magnifying glass.

My cell phone played Christmas songs to sing with Ruth. She remembered the words to numerous songs and sang with us, yet she could not remember what she had for lunch. A table or two away other voices joined in.

Was a miraculous cure for memory loss presented by singing Christmas carols?

Gary and Jerry started singing. We formed a new trio in the corner. The words to Silent Night came alive.

"You know, someday we`ll sing this song again— in heaven."

Gary slowly lifted his chin then it dropped again.

Jerry gave an empty stare.

"Will I see you in heaven, Jerry?" I asked.

He was silent.

Ruth asked, "Can I come home with you? I`m no trouble. I can help you."

Karen responded, "What can you do?"

"I can cook and help with chores."

"Who would take care of you? I work during the day. I can`t do all the things you need."

Ruth did not argue. "Will I see you again?"

"Yes."

"Tomorrow?"

"No, but we'll be back soon. We`re seeing the grandkids tomorrow." Karen gave her a hug.

"Kiss me."

Karen reached in to kiss her softly on her cheek.

"I love you," Ruth said.

"Merry Christmas. I love you too."

A hidden tear led us away to hope and pray all would someday find their way to heaven. I too, wanted to go home.

Do Final Words Matter?

Visits to Saint Louis allowed Karen and me to observe the family. My oldest brother Jim and his family cared for my ninety-year-old mother during her final days. I was not worried about her care as I watched my tough brother turn into a soft teddy bear.

"Mom, I'm gonna' give you a shot now. Is this place okay?" He gently touched her stomach. "You need to keep your feet elevated." He adjusted the rocker recliner to the proper height to help reduce her swollen leg. "Mom, you should try to eat something."

The visits gave us time to prepare. We knew Mom was tired of living and ready to go to her heavenly home.

She awoke and I asked her, "Do you want to watch the Cardinals?"

"I don't care. Watch what you want." She always watched the Cardinals.

"Do you want to play cards?"

"No, not now."

Those days of playing railroad rummy with her became a happy memory.

The final and most telling conversation took place the day I asked, "Mom, do you want to go to church?"

"Not today." This was a first. I still go to church because of my mom.

On a warm January day, we got the call. "It's Jim." Karen handed me the phone.

"How's Mom?"

"Not well. We've moved her to the Hospice facility. The nurse says it will be forty-eight hours or less. They're usually right."

"Karen and I will be there tomorrow."

We arrived in the late morning. "How's she doing?" I asked Jim.

"Her breathing is labored. I don't know how long she'll make it or if she'll wake up. I've called our brothers."

Alicia arrived with Owen. I met them in the Commons area as I wanted to discuss whether Owen should see Grandma Grape. As a toddler, Owen pronounced Grape when he was learning how to say "Grandma" as a toddler. The nickname stuck.

"Do you want to see Grandma Grape?"

"I want to see her walking in heaven."

Mom woke up one last time when her meal came. She did not verbally respond to conversation.

Jim asked, "Mom, do you want to eat something?"

My brother's wife, Karen asked, "Granny, do you want ice cream?"

Mom motioned toward the ice cream. Mom took a spoonful of ice cream and let it melt onto her tongue. I watched her throat contract slowly as the soothing ice cream flowed down her throat. She licked her lips for one last taste of sweetness. She savored that last supper as much as anyone I had ever seen.

Her head turned and she looked directly at each of us as she spoke her final words, "That sure is good!"

The next day at mid-afternoon, she gave a sudden heaving gasp. Her labored breathing was finished.

My brother Bob responded, "Is there something we can do?"

Later, alone in the room I kissed my mother on her cheek and felt her cold hands.

"No. There's nothing we can do."

My niece, Erica, entered the room.

"Where's her cross?" She looked around frantically, knowing its importance. She reached for the cross on the nightstand, then gently, yet firmly, unfolded my mother's hands and placed the cross into her fingers. Erica wiped her tears on the sleeves of her shirt.

My mother's final words were a metaphor of her life, great joy summarized so eloquently. "That sure is good."

Owen's words were of hope and faith. "I want to see her walking in heaven."

Erica's words were reflective of my mom's love of God. "Where's her cross?"

Bob's words showed compassion and love. "Is there something we can do?"

For Jim and his family, their actions and words spoke of loving compassionate care.

At the funeral, many spoke of the words my mother never said. She never cussed. She never said a bad word about anyone.

The final words of my mother will forever speak to us, giving hope of heaven and joy on earth. "That sure is good."

Justice Served

Kimanni was twelve when his mom called me.

"Tom, I need your help. I found out Kimanni skipped all his practices and games. His last game is tomorrow. Can you take him?"

Kimanni's mom had no car, and his dad was in jail.

"What time's the game? I'll make sure he's there."

I arrived at Kimanni's house in time for the Saturday game. "Where's Kimanni?"

"I don't know. He was here just a minute ago. I'll find him."

Was he hiding from me? Did he think he was in trouble?

He darted into the living room. "Hey, Kimanni. Where's your uniform?"

He looked bothered, raised his voice, "I don't need it."

"Yes, you do. You signed up for the team, and you're going to finish what you started."

"I don't need it. If you miss practices, you don't play."

"You're still part of the team. Get your uniform on. We need to go."

The drive to the field gave us time to talk. "Kimanni, I'm not going to ask you where you went after school. What's important is what you do from this day forward."

He sat and watched his team. For the past five years, Kimanni had attended every practice.

We made a deal to get him on a traveling basketball team provided he had no "D's. He was only able to attend two tournaments before the report card came. His coach said he had great potential.

Kimanni played junior varsity basketball and varsity golf during high school until an "F" his junior year stopped everything. Maybe his attention deficit disorder played a part in his grade. Regardless, he lost his eligibility to play basketball and transferred to a Christian school for his senior year.

Kimanni was of mixed race and none of the other teams we played had African American players. His coach counseled him not to over-react to any discrimination.

His coach was right. Kimanni was called several racial slurs prior to the Homecoming game. At one game, the opposing coaches refused to shake Kimanni's hand.

Homecoming gave us a chance to reach a five hundred winning percentage. During the last regular season basketball game, Kimanni scored thirty-three points. Everyone looked forward to a great Homecoming game.

The Eagles' fans filled the stands. The cheerleaders revved up the crowd. I wished we had a band.

Immediately the other team focused on stopping Kimanni. I commented to Karen, "They're going to double and triple team him the whole game."

We needed just one player to take the pressure off Kimanni.

Things were as bad as they could get with the score sixteen to one. Kimanni stole the ball for a breakaway and was a step ahead of the nearest defender. As he started to shoot the layup, the opposing player intentionally shoved him into a concrete wall. No foul? The crowd roared with boo's.

Kimanni recalled his father's advice. "If they hit you, hit 'em back. Knock 'em down."

But Kimanni turned away, ignoring the player and the referee.

I felt the injustice but was so proud of him for standing above his adversaries and not retaliating in anger.

During halftime, they prepped for the crowning of Homecoming King and Queen. Earlier I had asked Kimanni who he voted for.

With a broad smile he responded, "Who do you think?"

"At least you know you have one vote." He gave a confident chuckle.

They voted Kimanni Homecoming King. The kids at the Christian school were colorblind.

I felt like strutting around to tell everyone, "That's my boy." But he maintained dignity with a humble stride. For a few wonderful moments, I forgot the game.

The second half comeback began. We narrowed the lead to five. Our fans stomped their feet so hard the bleachers shook. The cheerleaders led the chorus, "Defense, defense."

The comeback was short-lived as Kimanni picked up his fourth foul. He sat on the bench while the margin spread to thirteen. Our crowd returned to silence.

With three minutes remaining, Kimanni returned for a three-pointer. "Get me the ball. Get me the ball."

Suddenly the crowd was back into it. The cheerleaders chanted again. I had to bend next to my wife's ear to be heard.

We held them again, and Kimanni hit another three from the corner. "Hurry guys. Hurry." Swish, he hit another three from the top of the key.

With seconds remaining, a teammate stole the ball and passed to Kimanni who made our last basket, another three. We were behind by one when the buzzer rang. The frantic finish occurred so quickly a fan asked, "Did we win?"

I replied, "Yes, he did."

Lost the game, only in points. Tears flowed down both cheeks as I hugged Kimanni at center court. "Kimanni, we had em. We had the momentum. You played great. You finished strong. You made four three pointers in four attempts when you got back in the game. We just ran out of time. I'm so proud of you!"

At a Homecoming game where his classmates conquered injustice, I watched a boy become a man.

Along with his peers, I declared Kimanni the Homecoming King.

Justice Appealed

Steve, the school superintendent, called. "Tom, I have Kimanni here with me."

"Is everything okay?"

"He`s fine. I wanted you to know before you heard or saw it in the newspaper. Kimanni was voted second team in the Western Valley Conference basketball team. I`m already trying to get this overturned, so please don`t do anything until you hear from me."

I thanked Steve and asked to talk to Kimanni.

"I`m sorry. We both know you should be first team. Are you okay? Do I need to come get you?"

"No, I`m fine."

Fine? My boy's been hurt and everything`s fine? How can he be so subdued in the face of such injustice? Has he been down this road before?

"We`ll talk later." I hung up and screamed in the car", "WWWH-HHYYY?"

A voice either in my own head or God`s voice answered, "Sin."

I had good reason to be upset. All year I followed the Iowa Athletic Association website. Within our conference, Kimanni was the leading three-point shooter, leading rebounder, second in scoring, and was the top defender with steals, rebounds and blocked shots. He deserved all-state recognition.

Was this a good old boy fraternity, racism, anti-Christian bias, or all of these? Calm down, Tom. Wait for Steve's call.

The next day Steve called. They would not reconsider. The voters saw Kimanni play only one time. He wasn't at summer camps or on select teams so nobody knew who he was.

I explained my plan to Kimanni. "I'm going to write an editorial to the Sioux City Journal." Kimanni was okay with the plan.

Then I called Steve. "I'm going to write the Journal about this injustice. I'll send you a copy. Let me know if I should change anything. I'll let our coach and Kimanni's mom see the editorial." I prepared the piece, and no one suggested changes.

The piece was submitted but never published. My calls to the editor were never returned. I met with Kimanni and asked him if he wanted me to go any further. He said, "No."

As a Caucasian, I had never witnessed racial prejudice firsthand.

Reality determines that statistical truth when untwisted is still truth.

Kimanni was worthy of being selected first team. He glorified me as his mentor. He also glorified God who is the ultimate judge.

Let the truth be known: Kimanni was not only first team, but also the player of the year for the Western Athletic Conference.

Say it often. It's the truth.

A Better Super Bowl

During the 2020 Super Bowl, my hometown Kansas City Chiefs came back from a seventeen-point deficit to win. Kimanni commented, "This may have been the greatest sporting event of all time."

What makes a sporting event worth remembering?

When Kimanni played football in the eighth grade his team came back from a twenty-four-point deficit to win.

These amateurs and their coaches executed the comeback to perfection. They even recovered an onside kick. Kimanni caught a crucial touchdown pass to seal the victory. That was nine years ago.

I can`t remember anything about the Super Bowl nine years ago.

When my daughter hit her first softball pitch after striking out so many times I cried. That gave me more satisfaction than watching future Hall of Famer Albert Pujols hit two home runs into the right field bleachers.

Who could forget Alicia's team's triple play when she was only six? It was the slowest and most chaotic triple play of all time. The bases were loaded. A fly ball was hit to our first baseman. She caught it with her foot on first base. The girl on first base didn`t tag up so that made two outs.

Half the fans in the packed stands yelled to their players to go back to their bases and the other half yelled to throw the ball to second or third for the out. The third out occurred in the middle of right field with the center fielder tagging the girl who tried to run to second base. Both players had no idea where second base was.

Our precious daughters united passionate competitive fans from both sides into laughter.

As a freshman, my son, Tom, scored a soccer goal against the varsity. It wasn`t supposed to happen.

I can`t remember any soccer goals from the professionals.

A sixth grader made a shot to force overtime at one of Tom`s basketball games. Sixth graders don`t often shoot from three-fourths down the court. They played three overtimes with the game ending in a tie — the greatest basketball game I ever saw.

Since retiring, I shot par golf once and got my first hole-in-one. I can`t tell which pro shot the last hole-in-one or the winning score at the last Masters tournament.

How can you compare these sporting events? If it`s the tear or laugh factor, sorry Patrick Maholmes, Albert Pujols, LeBron James, and Tiger Woods. All entertain for a time in their prime, but their primes don`t last forever. And they seldom bring us to laughter or tears.

But families bring tears and laughter that last forever.

Chapter Four

Spring

In Like a Lion

March 1, 2007, my first year working in Sioux City, Iowa. I lived across the Missouri River in a farmhouse outside Homer, Nebraska.

At ten a.m., my boss, Steve, came into the office I shared with my co-worker, Elizabeth. "The prediction is for a white out. It`s already snowing. Get out of here so you can take care of your family."

I had never been in a whiteout.

Elizabeth tidied up her desk. "I`m going home. Promise me you`ll leave soon. I grew up in Iowa, and I`ve seen whiteouts. They're nothing to mess with. Be sure to drive safely."

I offered the macho response. "Don't worry about me. I`ll get home fine. I have four-wheel drive."

That afternoon I was the only one who stayed at work. I had only missed one day of work in thirty years, and I was not sick, so I was staying. At five-thirty, I left the building.

In the parking lot, the first thing I noticed was the chill of a forty-mile per hour wind with a twenty-five-degree temperature. I jumped in and let the defroster take over.

Traffic was slow but still moving as I crossed the bridge from Sioux City to South Sioux City, then to Dakota City on highway 75.

Once out of Dakota City, I descended into the Missouri flood plain. Lots of farms and few trees. The winds had nothing to slow them down, other than my Tahoe. After I drove past Dakota City, I never saw another vehicle.

The howling wind blew the snow sideways. Visibility was thirty feet or less. With tense hands, I steered into the wind to maintain control. My eyes strained to see the road.

Would I hit someone? I could not see headlights.

I managed to reach my turnoff. Three miles west, three miles south and I would be home. I turned west and immediately fought the wind and snow.

The Tahoe stuck in a drift on the railroad tracks, a hundred feet from the highway. I backed across the highway. My foot squeezed the petal to accelerate. It didn't help. I was center-hung on the track's drift.

My wheels spun me into deeper trouble. I struggled to open the door against the fierce wind. The whiteout blew my glasses into the snow. I secured them tightly and went for the jack. It was March. My shovel was at home.

I pulled snow from under my vehicle. The storm replaced what I had cleared with new snow. My arms felt the weight of exhaustion.

Fear set in. My breathing intensified. Settle down, stop, and think. I returned to the front seat.

Would I die here? Would I kill someone else with a train crash? Maybe the train wouldn't crash and would destroy the Tahoe. Should I abandon the vehicle? Perhaps trains did not travel during white outs. Could I walk to safety? Did I have time before the next train?

There seemed to be no good answers. I felt helpless. "What haven't I done?"

A voice answered, "Pray."

"God, you've got to help me!" I prayed as if I could order God around.

Instantly, I heard a tap at the window. I hit the automatic window button. I could only see a portion of his cheek and pointed chin. He leaned in toward the top of my window.

"Try again. Drive slowly," he calmly said.

I paused a moment, waiting for the man to reach the rear and push. I gently pressed the accelerator and was suddenly free. It felt as if I was driving on a driveway.

No push or pull. My tires didn`t spin or slide. I saw no lights.

I threw the door open to thank him. He was gone.

Who saved me? Those words, "Try again" resonated in my mind. Someone was watching out for me.

The Master Gardener

It`s dead. I did it now. The garden's dead. We`ll have to re-plant.

My wife remained calm. "What happened?"

"I`m not sure. Maybe they burned up. All the plants are limp. I wonder if they couldn`t get enough oxygen. I`m sure it has something to do with the pool liner."

The root cause went back to an earlier time. We moved from Missouri to Iowa, and I switched the growing seasons. I planted in March instead of April.

The weather was mild, and everything came up fine. Then the weatherman predicted frost, but I had a solution.

I took our solar cover from the pool and stretched it over our railroad-tie gardens. The frost set in for several days.

Finally, a milder day came. I took the cover off. All the plants lay on their sides, still green but not healthy. Putrid green. Dead green.

Then I heard a soft voice in my head. "Breathe on them."

Now I`m not a superstitious person but I do believe in God. I had nothing to lose and everything to gain. I got on all fours and scooted around while breathing on each plant.

The next day the putrid turned a yellowish green. The dead came to life.

Ample water and sunlight provided a good combination for future growth.

Several months later the green garden became more than ripe tomatoes. It became a story to tell off the deck while eating grilled burgers.

Stay Good, Vernon

On March 10, 2019, I lost a neighbor and friend.

When I first met Vernon, my front door was open. He came over to check on me. Vernon immediately invited me to his church. We talked about hunting, something we had in common. Not many people are hunting at eighty-seven years old.

Vernon repeatedly told two stories. One involved his shot of a buck at over a hundred yards. The other involved a deer striking his vehicle on the way to church. Vernon complained to God about being a faithful servant, undeserving of such a hit. When he got out of the car, there was no damage.

On an early morning walk, Vernon waved me over to his driveway. He asked, "Do you remember how Jesus greeted Judas as 'my friend.' He wouldn`t have it any other way. He loved every one of us, even me."

Another morning, I told Vernon, "You know what I read this morning? The Bible says even in old age we can bear fruit." For Vernon and me, we were that biblical example. Iron sharpened iron.

On a hundred-degree day, I saw Vernon on all fours under a small apple tree. I went to check on him. He was picking weeds at the base of the tree.

Wow, will I be that fit at eighty-seven?

We wandered to the back of his house to sit and chat until sunset. Eventually our wives joined us. It was a simple event, not forgotten, not lived out enough. I left that evening telling Vernon, "Stay good."

We played cards with Vernon and Betty. With shifty eyes and a smile waiting for a laugh, he asked who should keep score. Vernon enjoyed laughter. Karen and I took Vernon and Betty to see Dennis Swanberg, a Christian comedian. We also saw several gospel concerts together. Our neighbors had become our friends.

When people ask me about Pleasant Valley, I tell them about Vernon, Betty, and their sixty-eight-year marriage. Vernon's yard was always pristine. He once told me his place was the prettiest place on earth. I think our Heavenly Father is proud of the yard and home Vernon built himself, including the furniture.

Vernon always led the prayer at the Pleasant Valley Seniors' Luncheon. He introduced me as, "This is my neighbor Tom. He's a good man." We joined in song and fellowshipped over food. Betty took care of the entertainment and food. She always prepared a plate of food for Karen who was working.

Vernon often told me he would be in heaven. He knew he had it right, at least by biblical standards about confessing sin, believing God forgave him, loving God, and loving your neighbor. He lived the words.

Vernon was a mentor, a friend, and a brother in Christ.

I miss him and I love him.

Stay good, Vernon. I'll see you in heaven.

Walk This Way

How can a two-year old teach me how to walk?

As I walked toward home on the gravel county road, my daughter pulled into the driveway with her son.

Two-year old Owen went into his airport run. He threw his arms around my leg. I reached down and grabbed his right hand as we continued our walk.

We came to the long driveway of our neighbor who lets us fish in her pond. Owen jubilantly explained, "Fishy this way." He tugged my arm then let go of my hand and pointed toward the pond. I convinced him to leave the "fishy" for another day.

Another neighbor's pasture adjoined the road.

"Look, Owen, a pasture."

He responded, "Cow". No cows, but we saw two horses.

Owen looked at me, "Daddy, Mommy, this way." He nudged my leg and pointed toward the horses. I persuaded him to continue our journey back home.

A puddle lay at the edge of the neighbor's driveway. A kaleidoscope of Tiger Swallowtails paused to drink. Owen ran into the puddle. The swarm erupted into flight. He reached to catch one but came away empty-handed.

We passed the neighbor's driveway. Owen noticed the dog near their home. "Dog this way."

"Owen, let's go."

Owen was no longer with me. I watched him pet the dog as if to say, *Slow down some, stop and love a little more.* The boy and the dog separated a minute later, content in time.

Owen taught me another way to walk: to pause, to enjoy life, to remember small creatures such as fish, cows, horses, and dogs. He taught me to marvel at and chase butterflies. Stop or slow down and love more.

"Owen, I had a wonderful time. Thank you. We'll do this again."

The Creek Speaks

What happens at the creek doesn`t stay at the creek. I cannot forget when I rescued my brother or when Charlie Brown saved my life at the creek. Even if I forgot, the scar on my left index finger lives with me every day to remind me.

In 1965, I ran from the creek.

I was ten and skinny as a beanpole. My seven-year old brother, Ron, was a solid fifty pounds. We were off to fish with a string and sticks. Hotdogs were the crawdads' bait. They grasped the hotdogs. We pulled them out and saved their tails to fish for catfish.

Ron spotted a large crayfish beyond the eight-foot string. He stepped in the shallow water to get a better cast. "Ron, you`re bleeding. Your foot is bleeding bad."

"What happened? Am I okay?"

I held his foot up. "You`ve cut the bottom of your foot." All I could see was blood.

Suddenly I felt as strong as Popeye The Sailor Man. I turned into an Olympic sprinter. My hundred-yard dash was timed at nine seconds, an adrenaline world record.

Despite the uphill run, I threw Ron on the kitchen table like an empty sock for Mom to examine. It turned out to be a long slice with a faucet full of blood. Mom stopped it with pressure. No stitches needed. No scar.

Ron was fine, but that was not my last dangerous creek adventure.

A year later, my best friend Charlie Brown and I threw dirt clogs at one another under the highway bridge that covered the creek. "It's raining. What are we gonna' do?"

"Charlie, we're safe and dry here. I don't have to be home until five. Mom knows I'm with you. We'll be fine."

Charlie looked at me. "It's raining hard. We'll get soaked if we run home."

The torrential rain turned into a Midwest monsoon. The six-inch creek was suddenly six feet deep and roaring fast. Sticks and logs moved much faster than boats on the Mississippi. Charlie grabbed a passing log and hopped on with me.

Our first canoe rides seemed fun until we headed around the bend to a sudden end. It was a logjam.

As we quickly approached, I asked Charlie, "What should we do?"

"Swim to shore."

"I can't swim."

Charlie swam the ten feet to shore.

I hoped to walk across the logjam. My log went under immediately, and my legs went with it. I reached my arms upward, holding onto the top of the jam. It was a pull up against the raging creek. The creek was winning. Strength faded fast. I thought I might drown.

"Help, help, Charlie help me!"

I grabbed a firm hold of the limb Charlie took from the logjam. He found that Hulk strength and won the tug of war.

Exhausted, gasping for air I caught a breath and said, "You saved my life."

On another day, I called, "Mom, I'm going to the creek. I'm gonna' try out my new knife and cut a notch into a tree for the snare trap."

"Be sure to always cut away from your body. Be safe. I love you."

As I used the knife to clear debris from the notch, I pulled the blade downward. The knife slipped from the wood into the second knuckle of my left index finger. Blood was everywhere. The cut was near the bone. I tried to control the bleeding with a handkerchief, but it turned red. I ran the quarter-mile home.

Dad and mom met me at the table. The cut looked like a one-inch wood shaving still attached to the piece of wood. Two of my brothers peeked from the basement door.

Dad was in charge. "Get me the rubbing alcohol." Mom ran to the cabinet.

He took his right arm and put me into a headlock. With his left hand, he pushed the flap of skin toward the bone and dipped my finger into the alcohol. My shock turned to searing pain as the alcohol penetrated my finger. I felt on fire. Tears were instantaneous to wash away the agony. My right arm flopped into the table's edge. I composed myself and gripped tightly to the edge of the table as Dad submerged the finger.

Loud laughter from the basement steps was eventually silenced by serious words. Jim said, "He's turning white as a bed's sheet. I think he might pass out."

My brothers knew the routine. No doctor. No emergency room. Dad spoke to me, "You'll be okay. You'll be fine."

I gave a final wince as he pressed the top of my finger with a wash-cloth bathed in alcohol. Then he passed my left hand to Mom.

She covered the top of the finger with thick white disinfectant as if she were frosting a cake. The cool ointment helped extinguish the burning sensation.

"Does that hurt?"

"It's getting better."

A gentler touch. My tears began to dry.

As she wrapped the gauze tightly, Mom spoke to me in a calm compassionate voice. "This might hurt a little, but you'll be okay."

In the hands of Mom, the pain disappeared.

She changed the bandage daily, but it was weeks before the finger healed. I was okay. I was fine. The one-inch vertical scar stretches to an end with a half-inch horizontal turn across my left index finger. I'm currently sixty-four years old and that scar has been with me for fifty-two years.

Despite it all, the joy of recollection makes me cry again. I miss them, Dad, Mom, and yes, even the creek.

Grandpa`s Wrong

In just two hours, I learned everything I was teaching my grand-children about garage sales was wrong.

For Heidi, Owen and Ian, this garage sale was their first.

"Today we`re going to learn how to negotiate."

Heidi gave me a puzzled look. "What's negotiate?"

"You will each get five dollars. When you find something you like, let me know. We`ll make an offer. They will either sell the item or let us know what price they think their item is worth. We can make another offer if you want. That`s negotiating."

Heidi began looking at some pink roller skates. She gave me a cute smile. "Can I have these?"

"You have five dollars. What are the roller skate's worth?"

"I don`t know."

"Do you want to offer them two dollars?"

Apparently, the woman in charge overheard my discussion. She came to assist. "There`s no charge for the skates."

No negotiations? Heidi thanked her.

We proceeded on to several more sales. Heidi had spent a buck twenty-five and now appeared to be an expert at managing her remaining account.

The boys were not as thrifty. They had two dollars left when the prize of prizes caught their eyes — remote control cars still in their original boxes. Remote cars run fifty to seventy-five dollars. After a long discussion, they each approached sheepishly yet convinced the cars were worth at least two dollars.

Anticipating rejection, I consoled them before they approached the owner.

Owen's lips curled a bit as he made eye contact with his coal black eyes "Can I have the car for two dollars?" Before the grey-haired woman could answer, Ian spoke up softly with sad convincing blue eyes.

"This is our last two dollars."

"Sure." Looking at me she said, "I really like what you're doing with these children."

Owen said, "Can we go now? I want to play with my car."

Ian supported Owen, "Ya, I want to play with my car too. Can we go?"

"We'll go in a minute or two. Be sure to thank this kind woman."

"Thank you. Thank you."

The events put me in a good mood. My daughter stared at a stack of name brand tennis shoes, longing to give them to children she works with. She estimated the value to be hundreds of dollars. I gave her forty dollars and they all became hers, to give and bless others.

When negotiating at garage sales, don't listen to Grandpa, but do take a grandchild.

A Sliver of Hope

It wasn't what I imagined. The prayer was simple. Don't let it rain Saturday at Crystal Cove Lake. The six boys from my Royal Rangers class needed to complete the field trip to earn their fishing merit patch. The Optimist Club scheduled Saturday to give each boy a fishing tackle box.

At three-thirty a.m., I woke to thundering rain. The hard rain continued when the alarm rang at six. I Googled weather on my cell phone. Green filled the entire screen. A closer look showed one sliver of emptiness the size of a pencil's point forty miles away.

A small sliver isn't much, but we held onto hope. Off to Wal-Mart Karen and I went to buy licenses, milk, and donuts. The downpour slowed. Windshield wipers adjusted. Rain became a drizzle as I dropped Karen off at church to prepare breakfast.

An intermittent drizzle led me to pick up the first three boys. To my surprise, five boys waited in the drizzling rain.

The drizzle continued through breakfast. Continuing my confident sense of hope, I opened the door to check the weather one last time. It was now a spitting rain.

Andy spoke for them all, "Can we go fishing? Can we go now? We're already wet."

They really want to go. At least the boys could get their free tackle boxes. Maybe there's no rain at Crystal Cove.

"Okay, but if it's raining we'll have to come back to the church." The boys ran to be first out the door.

We arrived at Crystal Cove. Still raining.

Eric noticed first. "Where is everybody?"

In a consoling voice I spoke, "They must have cancelled."

"Does that mean I won't get a tackle box?"

"Not today."

The church van turned into a chorus of "Aw."

"Let's go to the shelter and tie some knots. If it's still raining when we finish, we'll leave."

It was like a football huddle waiting for the play of the day. Each boy gave the knot-tying one good try. Some succeeded while others failed. We tied the final knot and left.

Stepping out of the shelter, I was surprised. The rain was over.

Andy shouted, "We're going fishing." He led the sprint to the dock.

We fished one hour. As we left the dock, it rained again. Sometimes a sliver of hope can calm a storm.

In Appreciation of Mom's

After a fishing day, I left with a greater appreciation of my wife and all mothers.

It was supposed to be a simple pleasurable morning taking six elementary-age children fishing. Four of them had never caught a fish. We brought three rods. Two rods were for the four boys and me. Karen took the other rod to fish with the other two boys.

Apparently, fishing was more popular than we envisioned. Thirteen children joined us on the short narrow dock. Thanks to my teacher wife, we established some basic rules: share without fighting, take turns catching fish and everyone needs to listen to Karen, Tom, and Isiah who's fished before.

Isaiah was the youngest and smallest of the group. Levi who was a head taller than Isaiah loved to bully Isiah. He enjoyed tackling Isiah at full speed when we played touch football. I worried how the two might get along.

It wasn't long before Josh had a trophy three-inch bluegill on dock. Then it began, "Tom, can you take the fish off the hook?"

Frank joined in, "Tom, he took my bait."

Zeke raised his voice, "Tom, can you bait my hook?"

With a calm voice, I said, "Just be patient."

When I baited Zeke's hook, I heard words I had never heard him say. "Thank you."

Then Levi said, "Isaiah's cool. He's helping me catch fish."

We witnessed patience, sharing, fun, joy, and smiles as wide as the lake. Four of the boys caught their first fish. The boys begged to come back the next day.

I felt anxious and struggled through the hour, hoping it would pass quickly. I worried the whole time about someone getting hurt. Karen said it was fun.

The refrain "Tom…Tom…Tom" echoed in my head. It was as if I heard a similar word, "Mom…Mom…Mom."

My mother raised four boys. For an hour fishing on a Saturday, I experienced what my mom experienced many days. She sacrificed her time for the children's time. She also managed to shop, clean the house, and have dinner ready on time every day when my father arrived home. She was precious to me.

Mom's do everything. They bring control to chaos and do it kindly, tenderly, patiently, and lovingly. They do it every day, usually with a smile.

Sometimes, I am consumed in my work and don't think about my children. I asked Karen, "Was there ever a day when you didn't think about your children?"

"No."

It was confirmed when I called my mom.

"Hi Tom, I was just thinking about you."

Mutual Joy

It was April 1, 2017 when I arrived at the Corp of Engineers land at Smithville Lake in Missouri. I scouted for a place to turkey hunt.

A tornado hit areas around Smithfield Lake on March 7. A country road showed a white shed's door in a tall tree, the piece speared by a pointed branch. On another road, the tornado took out a forty-yard path of trees like a sickle cuts weeds.

Proceeding down Short Road, I noticed a damaged church on cemetery ground. I pulled to the side of the gravel road, snapped pictures, and drove away.

Curiosity got the best of me. I turned the car around. To my surprise, this church damage was not from a tornado.

Right there was the grim reality of evil. Whoever did this came to rob, steal and destroy—to vandalize a church.

As I walked the basement floor, each step was slow and measured to avoid the broken glass. Nothing left behind in the sanctuary other than scattered animal feces.

Destruction continued outside. Someone tore away the door to an old outhouse. Near a fresh tombstone, the vandals twisted a wooden bench into a pretzel.

The tombstone read, "Father and Grandfather." A basketball player stood on one side of the words and a baseball player on the other. Dates revealed Larry was in his sixties — like me.

I paused a moment to give him respect, felt sad and distracted by the devastating damages. Others were near Larry as I walked the grounds paying respect, my mind focused on the idea that each soul had a greater story. Though the building was destroyed, everyone's soul legacy remained. My meandering took me back to Larry's grave.

I imagined the joy of a child's first birthday, a piece of cake across the face. The pride of a first grandchild, watching him grow to hit his first pitch, the last basketball shot through the hoop. What pride Larry must have felt with each accomplishment. His legacy lived on through pleasant memories.

The vandals came to rob, steal, and destroy. But Larry and I reminisced in joy.

Mom`s Testimony Lives

Mom is gone now, but her spirit lives inside others and me. My mother testified through her faith in God and her living for God. She didn`t preach a testimony. She lived it. Below is my attempt to thank her, to give her the praise and honor she deserves:

Mom, thank you for your unwavering faith. I saw this as you consistently took us to church every Sunday. You made sure we attended all confirmation classes. Seeds planted in me as a child, dormant for a time, were renewed by your persistent prayers.

I site you as the person when someone asks, "Who was the most influential person in your faith life?"

Mom, thank you for being orderly. You were outstanding at managing four boys of various ages. You fed us, drove us to events, and kept us clean from farm work. Meals, laundry, dishes, and vacuuming were always completed on time.

My jobs involved managing lots of files, which required multiple tasks within the files. I always strived to work timely and efficiently like you.

Thank you for your prayer life that continues today. In my own prayer life, I know God is real. He answers and provides for every need. Those answered prayers became my testimony.

Thank you for your worship. You showed me that worship is daily, monthly, and yearly. Church is a place to praise and honor God, to learn about God, and more importantly — a foundation for good living. Everyone saw God in your life both at church and away from church.

Mom, thank you for your service. When I think of the commandment to love others, I think of you. You were a remarkable woman who never verbalized faults in others.

My three brothers and I rose to honor you at your funeral. The Bible says, "Her children stand and bless her" (Proverbs 31 28 NLT).

We have become your living testimony.

Give God the Glory

With few words left, I looked at the prayer on my desk:

Father, I come to you humbly. Please forgive me. When I forget to understand, the words are in the master's hand. Gifts of words your artistry, now become my ministry, to touch the souls of humanity. Before I start today, it gives me joy to say, I give you the glory for our written story. Amen.

Faithfully, obediently, I continued to pray. A week later, I awoke in the night with several words God gave me. They were not a story, but a title. The story was for me to finish.

In life, I have been a giver and a taker. Through high school, my mother created words for my written assignments. Once a teacher praised me about a poem my mom wrote and wanted to read in front of the class. I took the credit.

In college, my best friend and Journalism major edited all my work to "A" level. I took the praise.

After college, I worked for twenty-eight years to own my two-car garage home in the suburbs. My happy life focused only on my wife, two children and me.

Happiness changed with a divorce and a downsizing company. A casino lifestyle only added to my unhappiness. I took excessive hours of time gambling and robbed my daughter of time I could have spent with her.

Although I took a twenty-five percent pay cut and lost our home, my life today is wonderful. To keep me from gambling, I volunteered. In 2013, Big Brothers Big Sisters awarded me Mentor of the Year.

I remarried and gave my life to Christ. Now I share my life with others. In giving, I find happy living.

God has always provided for my needs. When I focused on my needs by living my way there was something missing. After my divorce, I consistently read and studied the Bible. Reading the Bible gave me wisdom to raise my children and led me to what I was missing —living for God.

Living for God required me to have new priorities. My first was to love God and then others.

God talks to me through the Bible and prayer. Then I share his plan for my life through acts of service He leads me to complete. This is God's plan for happiness.

Why are we here? Simply to love God and others forever. The stories throughout this book happened only after I accepted Christ and let go of my past life.

My hope is that you find joy in reading the stories God inspired me to write. Perhaps through reading the stories you will be inspired to accept God's love and give him your life.

God, the stories you've given me, I now give back to you. Together, our artistry, our ministry, are now words to touch the souls of humanity.

Acknowledgements

The people and places of yesterday affect the words of today.

I believe perfect love came from my father and mother united with God. I am forever indebted to the firm foundation they each planted in me. Their patience in waiting for me to mature past alcohol, adultery, and gambling is so greatly appreciated. It`s obvious their prayers have been answered as each of these challenges are a thing of the past.

Charlie Brown saved my life when I was ten. An unnamed stuttering preacher at a one-room Baptist Church saved my soul. God knows who they are.

In school, Mr. Finnan made school fun and gave me hope that I could accomplish whatever I set my mind to. When I was sixty-four, Sally Jadlow taught me the basics of writing. These two people are encouraging gifts to the world. Sally remains a wonderful author with several published books.

John Morrell hired me when I was fifty-one and no one else wanted to interview me. Life sometimes takes us places we initially don`t want to go, but God has a better plan.

In Sioux City, Iowa, I became a Big Brother for Kimanni Thompson. Kimanni immensely changed my life. I love him as a son.

I want to especially thank the Big Brothers Big Sisters in the Siouxland area for allowing me to speak at fund-raisers. This is a wonderful organization, changing and impacting lives in a proven positive way.

I thought it best to involve Kimanni in the Royal Rangers. It was there I worked with Mic and Kevin, two incredible role models, not to mention my golfing friends. It was an honor to include a tribute to Mic while writing this book.

While working with the Royal Rangers kids, I learned what it is like to be poor. God was right by my side as I worked with these young boys watching each mature. May God continue to watch over each of them.

After sharing time with the Royal Rangers, I shared some time with hitchhikers, a prisoner, and a man with tattoos, the heart of Christmas and an angel. I learned how extraordinary each of them was. May God richly bless every one of them.

I'm forever thankful for family and friends that came to see Karen and I at our home in the dell. We continue to pray that with each visit they find peace and rest at our home.

My uncle Jesse spoke to us as young children. I never forgot the story of Jesus' worth to the world. Aunt JoAnn is inspirational to me with her unwavering faith.

Who could forget neighbors such as Doug, Modine, and Gail who shared her heavenly pond with us and brought joy to so many children? Farmer Doug was more than our repairperson. I always enjoyed a visit at his home and hoped to be invited in for some of Modine's fabulous cooking.

We were blessed over the years by Karla, Rusty and Tracey Lee who opened their homes and kept us grounded in the Lord.

Upon retirement, I took my Facebook entries of the past and introduced the rough drafts to the Kansas City Writers Group as well as to the Heart of America Christian Writers Network. These overwhelmingly gifted writers always encouraged and brought the best out of me.

I was introduced to RJ Thesman who is my coach and editor. She is such a gifted writer of many books who instilled in me the confidence to write the book while teaching me to hone my writing skills. Any writer should hire her.

Through it all, is the most incredible woman I know. My wife Karen continues to be the love of my life along with God. She shows me what love is every day through how she lives. Together with God, I know what a great marriage is.

God, where do I begin? Thank you for patience, forgiveness, and salvation. Thank you for the people and places that make these stories alive. Thank you for peace and joy. Thank you for faith, hope, and most of all love.

May God bless each of these people including anyone I have forgotten. I love them all.

About the Author

Tom Dickerson is a writer and speaker. When he was a Big Brother for the Big Brother Big Sister program, he spoke on their behalf on numerous occasions. In 2013, Tom was awarded the Iowa Big Brothers Big Sisters of the year award.

He holds a Bachelor of Science Degree in Law Enforcement Administration and a Bachelor of Arts Degree in Sociology from Western Illinois University. Tom was a kicker for the Leathernecks of Western Illinois. Before retiring in 2019, Tom worked various claims positions from claims manager to claims adjuster.

He is a member of the Kansas City Writers Group as well as the Heart of America Christian Writers Network.

In his spare time, Tom enjoys spending time with his grandchildren. He also likes to fish, hunt, golf, garden, and watch various sports.

He is happily married to Karen with a blended family of four: Alicia, Joy, Robby, and Tom.

He also has three grandchildren: Ian, Heidi, and Owen.

Tom continues to be a friend of Kimanni who he had the privilege of mentoring through the Big Brothers Big Sisters program.

Follow Tom Dickerson on Facebook at https://www.facebook.com/ or email him at TomDickerson07@gmail.com

www.ingramcontent.com/pod-product-compliance
Lightning Source LLC
Chambersburg PA
CBHW061146040426
42445CB00013B/1576